D1297983

Drama for Real Life

SIXTEEN SCRIPTS ABOUT THE CHOICES THAT SHAPE US

Steven James

IVP Books

An imprint of InterVarsity Press
Downers Grove, Illinois

InterVarsity Press
P.O. Box 1400, Downers Grove, IL 60515-1426
World Wide Web: www.ivpress.com
E-mail: mail@ivpress.com

©2006 by Steven James

All rights reserved. No part of this book may be reproduced in any form without written permission from InterVarsity Press.

InterVarsity Press® is the book-publishing division of InterVarsity Christian Fellowship/USA®, a student movement active on campus at hundreds of universities, colleges and schools of nursing in the United States of America, and a member movement of the International Fellowship of Evangelical Students. For information about local and regional activities, write Public Relations Dept., InterVarsity Christian Fellowship/USA, 6400 Schroeder Rd., P.O. Box 7895, Madison, WI 53707-7895, or visit the IVCF website at <www.ivcf.org>.

All Scripture quotations, unless otherwise indicated, are taken from are taken from the Holy Bible New Living Translation, copyright © 1996. Used by permission of Tyndale House Publishers, Inc., Wheaton, Illinois 60189. All rights reserved.

The names, characters, situations, events and places in this book are either the product of the author's imagination or are used fictitiously, and any resemblance to actual persons, events, or locations is coincidental.

Permission is granted to perform these sketches in noncommercial settings as long as one copy of this book is provided to each actor. If a ticket fee is charged for the performance, please contact InterVarsity Press for permission; guidelines can be found at <www.ivpress.com/info/permissions>.

Design: Cindy Kiple

Images: Yellow Dog Productions / Getty Images

ISBN-10: 0-8308-3341-2
ISBN-13: 978-0-8308-3341-2

Printed in the United States of America ∞

Library of Congress Cataloging-in-Publication Data

James, Steven, 1969-
  Drama for real life: 16 scripts about the choices that shape us /
Steven James.
    p. cm.
Includes bibliographical references and indexes.
ISBN 0-8308-3341-2 (pbk.: alk. paper)
1. Young adults—Religious life. 2. Youth—Religious life. 3.
Christian drama, American. I. Title
BV4529.2.J36 2006
246'.72—dc22

                                                                    2005022352

P	20	19	18	17	16	15	14	13	12	11	10	9	8	7	6	5	4	3	2	1
Y	21	20	19	18	17	16	15	14	13	12	11	10	09	08	07	06					

To Matt and Dana

CONTENTS

ACKNOWLEDGMENTS

Dozens of people helped read and critique these dramas as they were being developed. My thanks go out to each of them.

Special thanks go out to the drama team at Celebration Church, Blountville, Tenn.; the Crosspoint Company youth drama team at Bellevue Baptist Church, Cordova, Tenn.; Mark Collins and the Providence Academy class of 2005; Pam, Lara and Janette Johnson, Sunday Feathers, Alan McCartt, Sue VanEaton, Jason Sharp, Anne Carpenter, Esther Hathaway, Liesl, Ariel and Trinity Huhn, Ashley Vinson, Taylor and Kim Pruitt, Carly and Jane Altizer, Chris and Sonya Haskins, Laura Hendrix, Matt Stimmel, Steve Humphrey; Dick Major and the members of his Fundamentals of Acting class at Milligan College (Nick Barnes, Kory Drake, Crystal VanMeter, Becky Waruszewski, Diane Hostetler, Todd Davis, Lindsey Vogt, Amber Carderelli, Stephanie Dalton, Hannah Bader, Susan Daasch, Sarah Shepherd, Theron Humphrey, Corbin Geary, Mindy MacConnell, Courtney Terry, and Andy Frost) and Liz Dollar and the members of her acting class at King College (Katy Harlan, Lucinda Taylor, Reagan Cecil, Laura Hicks, Ashley Caire, Bradley Long, Lacey Kitchen, Amanda Coltrane, Jamie Barker, Katie Rawlston, Tasha McDaniel, Lindsay Adams, Luke McCall, Tad Giles, Amy Oblinger, Bradley Long). If I've forgotten anyone (as I probably have) please forgive me.

Thanks also to Cindy Bunch, Pamela Harty and Dave Zimmerman for your help, encouragement, guidance and patience.

INTRODUCTION

Dramas are not thinly veiled sermons. Sermons explain, dramas explore. Sermons define, dramas question. Sermons proclaim, dramas ponder. Sermons exhort, dramas expose.

The goal of a drama is not to solve a problem or even to make a point, but rather to tell a story or to raise an issue. Dramas can get under the skin of your listeners, and even though the situation or the story may be fictional, they can still speak the truth in a disarming way.

When people speak of theater, they often refer to "the suspension of disbelief." The idea is that we know the actors are pretending, the scenery is fake and the words are contrived, yet we accept it. We set aside our knowledge of the charade and believe in the story so that we can become emotionally engaged. Thus we suspend our disbelief.

Yet there's an important facet to this idea of suspended disbelief that often gets overlooked.

One night I was watching a war movie (it might have been *Cold Mountain,* I can't really remember), and as one soldier after another dropped dead, I realized something: *I'm gonna die.*

Yes, I already knew about death. I already knew I wasn't promised a thousand tomorrows and—as secure as life seems—death could catch up with me at anytime. I knew that. But the story helped me to finally believe it. Drama convinces us of the things we'd rather not believe. Stories help us accept what we already know.

Stories open our eyes so we can peer at the truth. Drama uses a pretend world to help us to better see the real one. And we need constant reminding. Because we know all sorts of things that we don't seem to believe: love conquers all, eternity is but a heartbeat away, sharing our faith is important, God cares about our problems.

Drama helps us to stop pretending and to start believing the things we already know. That's why we leave the theater breathing the air more deeply, noticing the sunset that spreads above us, valuing the light touch of our spouse's hand as we glide to the car. That's why we cry at the movies even though we know the stories aren't real. Because the truths of life and death and love and hope and romance *are* real. They resonate with our souls.

When we "suspend our disbelief" during a drama, we actually open ourselves up to finally *stop* suspending our disbelief in reality and—if only for a moment—to begin to truly *believe* the truths we already know.

The Next Generation of Church Dramas

Much has been written about our postmodern culture. Let me summarize a few characteristics of churches that are doing an effective job of reaching our emerging culture with the Christian experience. Typically, they tend to have these three characteristics.

They tell the truth by telling stories. The emerging generations want to discover meaning for themselves rather than be told what they're supposed to believe. They'll engage with the message more intimately when stories are used at the heart of the teaching experience, not just as illustrations to liven up the sermon. In addition, people today are very narratively astute. They'll make connections between stories, images and metaphors without having the application spoon-fed to them. Connections don't always need to be spelled out and explained. That's why you'll notice that some of the dramas in this book have several stories converging or a group of people all presenting monologues that weave together. This mosaic approach to storytelling is effective in our emerging culture because of the next generation's keen understanding of story.

They foster honest communities. Too many people in our culture have been shown a caricature of Christianity. If we're going to invite folks to experience genuine Christianity, we need to be honest about what it really involves. Our dramas and worship services need to tell the truth without watering down the issues or showing only an idyllic version of the Christian life. That doesn't mean we hammer people with guilt trips; it just means that we use honesty to get to the heart of the matter and stop pretending we're so perfect. Honest dramas are always preferable to moralistic, preachy ones. For that reason you'll find dramas in this book that deal with real issues such as marital affairs, materialism, death, temptation and suicide in an honest, upfront way.

They create experiential worship. Many people today equate truth with experience. So when they say, "That's not true for me," they mean "I haven't experienced that in my life." One way to help people encounter God is to create worship services that appeal to the senses, provide opportunity for individual involvement and weave music, imagery, poetry and drama together to touch not just the intellect but also the imagination and the heart. This collection includes a number of dramas that do just that.

How to Use This Book

Over the years I've found some directors who want as much freedom as possible in producing church dramas, and others who want notes and tips for each script to make the sketch as easy as possible to produce and perform. As I was working on this book I decided to err on the side of clarity. As you read through these scripts you'll notice that I tried to provide as many tips and suggestions as possible. I did this not to stifle the imagination of the most creative directors but to provide help for the more inexperienced.

Each drama in this collection includes simple stage directions. However, the ministry and performance venues at different churches vary greatly. Some drama ministries have a huge stage, cutting-edge technical capabilities and professional actors; other ministries are performing in basement fellowship halls on Wednesday night. So take the staging and blocking suggestions as a jazz singer might take a melody. Use them, improvise and create a new melody that takes the music to the next level.

Every script also includes tips, audio-technical suggestions and (in appendix three) a list of suggested segues to move from the drama to the message. Each script also includes minute-by-minute time markers to provide an estimate of the length of the drama.

At the end of this book you'll find several appendixes with more detailed information for actors and directors. You'll also find a number of indexes to help you find the right sketch for your event. The cast index lists the number of male and female cast members needed for each drama; the Scripture index will help you find dramas that relate to specific Scripture passages, and the topical index lists dozens of topical connections to the scripts in this book.

Most of the scripts use a small number of actors, simple props and no costumes. If no specific costume suggestions are given, have your actors wear casual contemporary clothes. Use general stage lighting and lapel (or headset) microphones, unless otherwise noted.

Some playwrights are very touchy about people changing any of the words in their scripts. And while I've taken great care in crafting the words used in these dramas, I trust you to work with your actors to create the most effective presentation possible. You know your actors and your audience better than I do.* So if a certain phrase or specific wording doesn't work well, feel free to adapt it slightly and make minor script revisions. You can also change names of places and characters if you wish. However, please don't tinker with a sketch in such a way that you change its overall flow or theological intent.

Today more and more churches are videotaping dramatic performances and then showing the video during worship. In some cases this is helpful. For example, my church has a Saturday evening service and three Sunday morning services. We use all volunteer actors and directors. So if you volunteer to act in a sketch, you're volunteering to give up a big chunk of your weekend—Saturday

---

*A number of words (audience and performance being among them) tend to carry negative connotations in some Christian circles. An audience is simply a group of listeners, and a performance is what you do for them. Jesus performed his stories to audiences just as we do today. Please don't get hung up on the terms; they're the simplest and least confusing terms I know of in the realm of drama ministry.

night and Sunday morning. The thought of recording the drama on video and then playing it during worship is attractive.

However, we almost always prefer live performances. Why?

Live performance is interpersonal. It occurs within and enhances community. It's not just an event people watch, it's a shared experience.

In addition, videos and films are poorly edited, scripted and directed at many churches. If you have the ability to produce high-quality videos that won't look cheap and cheesy, go for it. But if you don't, please don't. People will naturally compare the videos they see at your church with the videos they see during the rest of their lives. Only use videos if you can produce quality work.

Some churches have started to shy away from using dramas in lieu of having people tell true stories (testimonies) of what God is doing in their lives. Certainly testimonies are a welcome and very biblical addition to contemporary worship; however, there's no need to discard drama and fictional stories.

As far as we know, none of Jesus' parables were factually true. (They may have been based on actual events, but we don't know.) Yet no one ever called him to task and said, "Hey! Did that really happen? Did a priest and a Levi really ignore a hurt guy by the side of the road? Did a guy named Lazarus really get carried to heaven on angel's wings?" The people didn't question Jesus because they knew that even if his stories weren't historical events, they spoke the truth. Dramas do the same.

So, work toward weaving both testimonies and dramas into your services and keep using live drama even as you explore the technological frontiers of film and video.

Enjoy!

PART ONE

BELIEFS

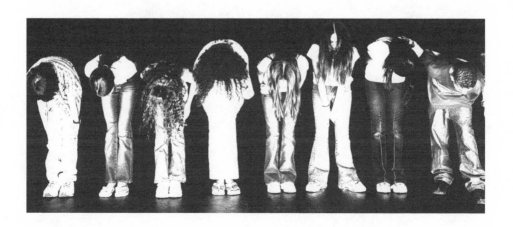

1

NOT WHAT I EXPECTED . . .

Instead, they were longing for a better country—a heavenly one. Therefore God is not ashamed to be called their God, for he has prepareda city for them.

HEBREWS 11:16 NIV

Diane arrives in the afterlife and is soon discouraged. It's not really what she was hoping for. But when she complains enough, she discovers a distressing truth. This disarming drama will help reveal misconceptions people have about heaven and hell.

Time: 5 to 6 minutes

Cast

DIANE   a typical twenty-something woman who has just arrived in the afterlife

GUIDE   (male), the worker assigned to new arrivals

Costumes: The guide is dressed in bare feet and a white choir robe. Diane is wearing a casual outfit of blue jeans, a t-shirt (stained with blood), comfortable shoes and a jacket or vest (hiding the bloodstain).

Props/set: a clothing rack with five or six white choir robes, a clipboard with papers, a pen, an ATM card

Technical needs: general stage lighting (bright) and two lapel or headset microphones

Tips: This sketch depicts the stereotypical views of heaven that many Christians hold. It would be great for setting up a message about what heaven is really like. Be sure your speaker takes the time to clarify what the Bible says heaven and hell are *really* like!

Each time Diane and her guide move to another "room," they just move to another place on stage and motion toward another imaginary door. They end their tour next to the hanging choir robes. If desired, have "heavenly" sounding harp music playing in the background. Be sure Diane's jacket hides the bloodstain on her shirt until she takes it off later in the sketch.

■ ■ ■

A hallway with lots of doors and rooms. At the end of the hallway (which is imaginary) hang the white choir robes (which are real). As the lights come up, DIANE and her guide enter the stage. DIANE is awed by her surroundings. The GUIDE is carrying a clipboard.

DIANE *(looking around)* Hey, I really appreciate you giving me this tour . . . I mean, having just arrived and all.

GUIDE Of course, that's my job.

DIANE *(looking around)* Ah . . . I can't believe I'm finally here!

GUIDE Yeah, it usually takes a while to sink in. *(walking toward center stage and gesturing off to the side)* And this . . . is the harp room!

DIANE The harp room? *(thinking about it for a moment)* Oh, yeah, harps, harps. Of course!

GUIDE *(glancing at his clipboard)* We have you signed up for practices every day from 2 to 4.

DIANE But, um, I don't . . . I don't play the harp.

GUIDE *(chuckling)* Well, you'll have plenty of time to learn, now, won't you?

DIANE I guess so.

GUIDE We love our harp music here.

DIANE Um, I'm not really a big fan of harps. I'm kinda more into techno-rock and some of that Celtic folk music stuff. *(hopefully)* Any chance of picking up guitar lessons instead?

[One-minute mark]

GUIDE *(glancing down at a clipboard)* I'm sorry, we have you down for harp lessons . . . and I doubt we made a mistake! *(elbows her as if he just told an inside joke)*

DIANE Yeah, right.

GUIDE *(moving to another part of the stage)* And over here we have the choir rehearsal rooms!

DIANE Choir? You gotta be kidding! I couldn't carry a tune in a bucket!

GUIDE	Well, I guess you'll have a little work to do before you sing for the Big Guy, huh?
DIANE	*(mumbling)* No one told me I had to sing . . .
GUIDE	*(moving across stage again, gesturing toward another "room")* And here we have the recitation rooms.
DIANE	Recitation rooms? As in memorizing stuff?
GUIDE	Well, yes. There's a certain number of verses you'll be asked to learn each week. And of course we have periodic performance exams . . . so you'll want to keep up.
DIANE	Memorizing verses? That's rough. This place is gonna be a lot of work! Oh well, I guess I'll get used to it.
GUIDE	Perhaps . . . *(gesturing to another part of the stage)* And of course, in this room we have your treasures and rewards. Just like you wanted.

[Two-minute mark]

DIANE	My rewards?
GUIDE	Yes. You've been storing up treasures here for quite some time. We used to be on the gold standard, of course, but we've recently upgraded to an ATM system. Cash on demand. Here. *(hands her an ATM card)* Just swipe and enjoy.
DIANE	All right! Now that's something I was looking forward to! Um, how much do I have in my account?
GUIDE	More than you could ever need. And any time you want more, all you have to do is ask.
DIANE	Wow! I guess I'll be able to put up with the harp and the choir and the memorizing after all. An unlimited bank account. I'm rich! You should have seen my place back on earth.
GUIDE	I did.
DIANE	Oh, yeah. Of course. Anyway, it wasn't anything to write home about—but now I can afford the best place money can buy! Marble floors, crystal chandeliers, maybe some cute little pearly gates out front.
GUIDE	*(off-handedly)* Of course, there's no place to spend it.
DIANE	What?
GUIDE	Your treasures. Your wealth. There's nowhere to spend any of it.
DIANE	You mean . . . I've got an unlimited supply of cash and nothing to spend it on?

GUIDE	Exactly.
DIANE	But what good is it then?

[Three-minute mark]

GUIDE	You can make little bonfires, wallpaper the hallways, maybe rip up the bills to make confetti for special occasions. That's always fun.
DIANE	*(exasperated)* This is nuts!
GUIDE	There's no buying or selling here. Everything you need is provided . . . Well, that about wraps up the tour. Why don't you get settled in?
DIANE	But don't I get wings and a halo or something? What about my own little private cloud somewhere?
GUIDE	I'm sorry. That only happens in Hollywood. Oh, one more thing, though . . . *(handing her a choir robe from the rack)* here's your robe.
DIANE	Robe?
GUIDE	Yes. All rookies are required to wear a robe.
DIANE	What about my jeans? And these cool shoes? This is my favorite outfit! *(taking off her jacket, she notices some bloodstains on her t-shirt)* Except for the blood here on this shirt . . . *(brushes away at the bloodstains)*
GUIDE	I'm sorry. You wouldn't want to be wearing that when you meet the Big Guy, would you?
DIANE	I don't know . . . I . . .
GUIDE	And of course, we can't have the others being envious, now, can we? . . . *(turning to leave)* I'll see you at 2 o'clock for your first lesson.

[Four-minute mark]

DIANE	You're my teacher?
GUIDE	*(smiling)* Oh, I love harp music.
DIANE	*(mumbling)* Oh, great . . . *(remembering something)* Hey, wait a minute. You said I got here as a result of a car accident, right?
GUIDE	That's right.
DIANE	Well, what happened to my husband? I mean, we'd just gotten back from our honeymoon. He was in the car too. That much I remember.
GUIDE	*(looking through the papers on his clipboard)* I'm sorry. He didn't make it.

DIANE   *(suddenly serious)* What do you mean he didn't make it?

GUIDE   Oh, he died all right. But he didn't make it here.

DIANE   You mean?

GUIDE   *(nods)*

DIANE   *(distraught)* Oh, no! I can't believe it! You're sure?

GUIDE   *(nods)*

DIANE   I don't understand . . . You don't think maybe I could see him for a few minutes, you know, just to say goodbye?

GUIDE   I'm sorry, that's strictly forbidden.

[Five-minute mark]

DIANE   Yeah, right . . . Listen, I gotta say, this place isn't really what I had in mind. I mean, it seems like there's an awful lot of obligations—what with learning the harp and memorizing verses and rehearsing for the choir—and none of this is stuff I like to do! And here, what about this? *(touches her side where the bloodstain is)*—ouch! How come my side still hurts?

GUIDE   You were in a terrible accident.

DIANE   Yeah, but I'd always heard that up here there isn't supposed to be any pain or suffering or stuff like that . . .

GUIDE   That's what they say—

DIANE   —Just peace and joy—

GUIDE   —About heaven.

DIANE   *(startled)* Huh?

GUIDE   You know, heaven—the place your husband ended up. C'mon now, get changed. The Big Guy is waiting to meet you. It's time for you to get moved in.

Freeze. Fade out.

2

THE COMMENTATOR

Why do you call me, "Lord, Lord," and do not do what I say?

LUKE 6:46 NIV

When Jerod explains his process for applying what the Bible says, Alicia is shocked. But when she tries to confront him, the tables are turned and she realizes something uncomfortable about her own relationship with God. Use this drama to explore what it really means to follow Jesus.

Time: 5 to 6 minutes

Cast

ALICIA (mid-twenties), a thoughtful woman who believes she's doing pretty well following Jesus

JEROD (mid-twenties), Alicia's studious friend who tends to be selective in his interpretation of Scripture

Props/set: eight or ten Bible commentaries, notebooks, Bibles, a couple comfortable coffee shop style chairs, a table or desk, a couple of coffee cups (if desired)

Technical needs: general stage lighting and two lapel or headset microphones

Tips: If you use a desk or table, make sure that the characters still remain visible to the audience. Don't get too stuck behind the table. Feel free to have the characters stand up and walk around. Don't let the studious aspect of this sketch hinder your imagination when it comes to blocking this drama.

■ ■ ■

A local coffee shop. 4.00 p.m. As the lights come up and the scene opens, JEROD is on stage seated at a table (or desk) studying a bunch of Bible commentaries. Then, ALICIA enters and the scene gets rolling.

ALICIA Hey, Jerod!

JEROD Hey, Alicia.

ALICIA	What'cha doin'?
JEROD	Oh, this is great stuff. I'm teaching that Bible study on Wednesday nights, right?
ALICIA	Right.
JEROD	Well, I'm checking what all these different commentators have to say about the verse we're studying.
ALICIA	*(sitting down, joining JEROD)* Cool. So, what verse is it?
JEROD	Well, right here, *(points out the verse in the Bible)* Luke 9:23, where Jesus says, "If anyone would come after me, he must deny himself and take up his cross daily and follow me." *(NIV)*
ALICIA	*(thoughtfully)* Hmm. So, what does it mean to follow Jesus?
JEROD	Yeah. *(holding up a commentary, speaking quickly)* Klugelman here says this verse is a reference to the Jewish cultural norms of the day speaking about how Christ was referring to abandoning the confining structures of the Jewish higher caste system to follow him into a new sociopolitical order!
ALICIA	Huh?

[One-minute mark]

JEROD	*(grabs another commentary, quickly)* But Franzheimer disagrees. He says Jesus is really referring to the more traditional Christocentric contextual implications of a neo-archetypical rabbinic reinterpretation of Old Testament laws!
ALICIA	I have no idea what you just said.
JEROD	Neither do I! Isn't this great! The more I study, the less I understand any of it!
ALICIA	Wow! By this time tomorrow you won't know anything at all.
JEROD	*(distracted)* Yeah, it's awesome, huh!
ALICIA	*(unimpressed)* Yeah, awesome . . . Those commentaries really make the Bible sound complex.
JEROD	Yup. I'm hoping to memorize a few of these explanations by Wednesday night. Really impress people. This one girl, Julie, she really likes smart guys.
ALICIA	Jerod!
JEROD	But that's not even the tough part.
ALICIA	What *is* the tough part?

JEROD	Now I gotta make all the blanks in my outline start with the same letter. I think I'm gonna use "D" this week . . . Let's see . . . D . . . D . . . D . . .
ALICIA	But, Jerod, did you ever think it might just mean what it says?
JEROD	Huh?
ALICIA	You know, mean what it says. Deny yourself and follow him. Couldn't it just mean that?

[Two-minute mark]

JEROD	Deny! That's good! Good D-word, Alicia! Deny!
ALICIA	You weren't even listening to what I said, Jerod! Deny yourself and follow him. Couldn't it just mean that?
JEROD	Well, I guess it could . . . I mean, I suppose. I'd need a little more research to figure out if that's what the author is really getting at.
ALICIA	What the author's really getting at?
JEROD	Yeah.
ALICIA	It doesn't really seem that tough to me: Say no to yourself and yes to Jesus.
JEROD	Well, that's your interpretation.
ALICIA	It's not an interpretation! I'm just reading what it says!
JEROD	Oh yeah? Well how are we supposed to follow him today when we can't even see him?
ALICIA	Um, I'm not sure exactly.
JEROD	And he doesn't mean to pick up a literal cross does he?
ALICIA	Well, no.
JEROD	OK, then.
ALICIA	OK, but he means we should do what he said. Like be holy, be pure, be perfect, sell all we own and give to the poor.
JEROD	Jesus didn't really mean "sell everything you own and give it to the poor."
ALICIA	He didn't?
JEROD	Of course not. It was a form of speech called hyperbole, which is exaggeration with the intent to make a point.
ALICIA	Really?
JEROD	Yeah.

[Three-minute mark]

ALICIA   Oh. What did he mean when he said *(flipping a Bible open to the book of Luke)* . . . here: "Give to everyone who asks you, and if anyone takes what belongs to you, do not demand it back"? *(Luke 6:30 NIV)*

JEROD   You have to look at that in context.

ALICIA   *(flipping to the book of John)* How about in John 12:25: "The man who loves his life will lose it, while the man who hates his life in this world will keep it for eternal life"? *(John 12:25 NIV)*

JEROD   Jesus is a man of love; he doesn't want us to *hate* anything.

ALICIA   I see. Well, what about in Luke 14 when he said that anyone who doesn't carry his own cross and follow Jesus can't be his disciple? *(Luke 14:27 NIV)*

JEROD   Oh, he's using vivid imagery to show that following him isn't always easy. It's difficult . . . *Difficult* starts with a D!

ALICIA   How about that. I never realized how practical and sensible Jesus was.

JEROD   *(writing in your notebook)* Yup.

ALICIA   I always thought he was more radical and revolutionary.

JEROD   Um. Well, he is . . . I mean.

ALICIA   I see. It's so much clearer now.

JEROD   Good.

ALICIA   *(sarcastically, getting up to walk around)* So pretty much Jesus never really meant what he said, he only meant what you say he said.

[Four-minute mark]

JEROD   Look, Alicia, why are you getting so snippy?

ALICIA   It's just that instead of applying the simple things Jesus says, you're making excuses for not doing them!

JEROD   Doing them! *Doing* starts with D!

ALICIA   Jerod, stop it! A follower of Jesus is someone who does what he says. It's that simple.

JEROD   *(standing up)* Oh, really?

ALICIA   Yes.

JEROD   Have you sold all you own and given the money to the poor?

ALICIA   Huh?

JEROD	Are you pure? Or holy? Or perfect?
ALICIA	Well . . .
JEROD	Or given money to every homeless guy who asks you?
ALICIA	Um, no.
JEROD	Or let people wrongfully take stuff from you and then not demand it back?
ALICIA	That's not the point—
JEROD	Do you really hate your life, like he said? Do you always say no to yourself and yes to him? Do you really pick up your cross and give up everything you own?
ALICIA	No . . . I guess I don't.
JEROD	Then why are you criticizing me? I mean, c'mon, Alicia. You said it yourself: a follower of Jesus is someone who does what Jesus says. And you don't do it.
ALICIA	Well, um . . .

[Five-minute mark]

JEROD	You can't take him literally. No one does anymore. At least I'm not saying one thing and doing another. At least I'm being practical. At least these commentaries help me with that.
ALICIA	But that's not how we're supposed to—
JEROD	Look, no one does what Jesus said. No one lives like that. It just wouldn't work in our world. I mean, imagine what the world would be like if we really took him literally!

After a pause

ALICIA	*(thoughtfully, convicted)* Huh. Yeah. Imagine that.
JEROD	Well, I gotta get back to my studying. See ya later.
ALICIA	*(distracted)* OK . . . See ya. *(thoughtfully, as she begins to walk away)* Yeah. Imagine that.

Fade out.

3

ASTRAY

But now, O Israel, the LORD who created you says: "Do not be afraid, for I have ransomed you. I have called you by name; you are mine. When you go through deep waters and great trouble, I will be with you. When you go through rivers of difficulty, you will not drown! When you walk through the fire of oppression, you will not be burned up; the flames will not consume you. For I am the LORD, your God, the Holy One of Israel, your Savior."

ISAIAH 43:1-3

Mika feels desperately alone and has started to consider suicide as a solution for her problems. Interspersed throughout her monologue we hear the comments of her guardian angel and his associate as they try to help her. They can't believe how quickly she has forgotten how precious she is to God. But will they think of a way to help her before it's too late?

Time: 7 to 9 minutes

Cast

MIKA (female), a lonely, suicidal twenty-year-old

ADEK (preferably male), Mika's guardian angel who wants desperately to help her

NATAL (male or female), a young cohort angel who has come to discuss Mika's situation

MRS. BINGHAM (sixty-ish), a grandmotherly woman who befriends Mika

Costumes: Mika is dressed in typical college student attire. The angels are dressed distinctive. Something cool, hip.

Props/set: a set of porch steps in front of Mika's apartment, a purse, a pair of scissors (inside the purse—the scissors should look very sharp but not be sharp enough to injure the actress)

Technical needs: General stage lighting and four lapel or headset microphones. If desired, alter the lighting when the two different groups are talking: a more diffuse, general stage light when the angels are talking, and a tighter spot on Mika when she's talking.

Tips: As you work on your blocking and movement, explore whether or not you want the angels and Mika to freeze while the others are delivering their lines. It may work well to let them freeze. If however, you choose to let Mika continue to move, she must stay oblivious to the angels. Throughout the drama the angels might even touch her tenderly on the shoulder or hair, but she remains unaware of them.

Be sure that your actors know how to pronounce Mika's name: "Mee'ka," rhyming with "beak-a."

Because of the graphic nature of certain portions of this sketch, use discernment when performing this drama with young children present.

■ ■ ■

MIKA is on center stage, seated on the steps to her apartment as the lights come up and the scene begins. She has her purse on her lap. The angels step out of the shadows shortly after the lights come up.

NATAL	So, is this her?
ADEK	Yeah.
NATAL	What's her name again?
ADEK	Mika.
NATAL	Pretty. Russian?
ADEK	Yeah.
NATAL	Appropriate too.
ADEK	Yeah.
NATAL	So, how is she?
ADEK	Not good.
NATAL	*(looking at her more carefully)* What, um, what have you done for her?
ADEK	All I can. It's hard, though. She's fighting it. Every time. Every step of the way.
NATAL	So . . . what do we do next?
ADEK	Honestly, I don't know.

The angels freeze or step into the background, change lighting to a tight spot on MIKA.

MIKA *(to the audience)* Here, in the city where I live, hardly anyone looks at you, not really. They just brush past you on their way to . . . whatever. If you even make eye contact they get suspicious.

[One-minute mark]

(after a pause) I saw my neighbor from across the street, Mrs. Bingham, walking her dog again this morning. I see 'em almost every day when I leave my apartment. She waves at me sometimes. Mrs. B, does. I've only really talked to her, like, a couple times. I wonder what she thinks of me? I wonder if she even knows my name?

Broaden the spotlight as the angels step back into the light.

ADEK You see?

NATAL Yeah, I do.

ADEK So.

NATAL Has she forgotten, or didn't she ever know?

ADEK She knew. She knew. She forgot.

NATAL But how?

ADEK The same as most of the ones who forget. Slowly. Drifting. Caught in the waves—

NATAL One ripple at a time.

ADEK Yeah. One ripple at a time.

The angels step into the background; change the lighting to a tight spot on MIKA.

MIKA There's this homeless guy near the coffee shop where I work. He's always smiling and hugging people, introducing strangers to each other. "Friend?" he asks, and they can tell he's, well, you know, "special." So they smile and say, "Yeah, friend."

Then he tries to get 'em to hug each other. It'd be funny if it wasn't so tragic. They almost always pull away.

(after a pause) He always tells me I'm beautiful. "You don't know who you are!" he says. *(sarcastically)* Yeah. Who I am.

[Two-minute mark]

29

Mrs. B. didn't walk her dog today. It was foggy and cold out. I could hear the dog clawing at the gate as I walked past. Barking. Trying to be free. Trying to get out.

Broaden the spotlight as the angels step back into the light.

NATAL   *(walking around MIKA)* I can't stand seeing 'em like this. Have you tried to remind her?

ADEK   Yes, of course. In little ways.

NATAL   The neighbor, Mrs. Bingham?

ADEK   Yes.

NATAL   The homeless guy? Is that you too?

ADEK   Yeah. I've tried to remind her, to show her who she really is. But *(waving his hand in front of her face)* it's almost like she's blind to what matters. To what's really real.

NATAL   That's what happens when they forget.

ADEK   Yeah. I know.

The angels step into the background.

MIKA   *(gets up and walks around for this section, but stays in the light.)* We used to have a dog—back when I was, like, nine or ten—this stray dog who always followed me home. My big brother would kick it in the side. Hard. "Git outta here!" he'd say.

[Three-minute mark]

I wanted to help the dog, but I didn't know how. I didn't know what to do . . . And the dog didn't leave. It just kept coming back. And he kept kicking it. The stupid mutt kept hanging around our house. Maybe it was looking for a place to fit in. Maybe it had nowhere else to go. Then one day we saw it in the ditch near our driveway. It'd been hit by a truck or something. On its way to our house so that my brother could kick it . . .

That's how I feel sometimes. Like that stupid dog. Trying to fit in. Even if it means getting kicked in the gut. Anything not to be a stray anymore.

Broaden the spotlight as the angels step back into the light.

NATAL   Are you sure she knew?

ADEK   I was there when it happened.

NATAL   Hmm.

ADEK	She knew.
NATAL	I'll never understand how they can forget so quickly, so easily.
ADEK	It's in their nature.
NATAL	Is it?
ADEK	I've heard that it is.
NATAL	*(looks into MIKA's eyes, or places his hand on her shoulder.)* We have to do something for her.

[Four-minute mark]

The angels step into the background; change the lighting to a tight spot on MIKA.

[This is the beginning of an optional section. If time is a constraint, you could eliminate this 2.5 minute section.]

MIKA	My life wasn't all that bad growing up. I was just a normal kid, you know. Trying to fit in, belong, find my way, figure out my place in the world. But it never seemed to work.
	I always got Bs in school. Just good enough to avoid attention. Always good enough to slip through the cracks. Average.
	C is supposed to be average. A is excellent, B is good, C is average, D—poor, F—flunking. So you'd think most people would get Cs, right? Most people would be average? But they inflate the grades. Everyone knows they do. So, like, everyone gets at least a B. I guess that means we're all good. It's so we feel good about ourselves. Have a high self-esteem.

Broaden the spotlight as the angels step back into the light.

NATAL	*(getting frustrated)* I don't know whose idea this whole self-esteem thing was.
ADEK	I do. I know.
NATAL	It wasn't—
ADEK	Yes.

[Five-minute mark]

NATAL	Are you sure?
ADEK	I have it on good authority.
NATAL	I should have known. It only hurts them, doesn't it?
ADEK	It keeps 'em focusing on themselves.
NATAL	*Self*-esteem.
ADEK	Right.
NATAL	*(looking around)* It's a backward world here, isn't it?

ADEK   Yes. It is.

NATAL   They think it's all about them. They're in love with themselves. Trying so hard to feel good—

ADEK   About them*selves.*

NATAL   Yeah.

The angels step into the background; change the lighting to a tight spot on MIKA.

MIKA   *(sits down again)* So then, I guess everyone's above average. I mean, how many straight-C students do you meet? Think about that one for a while. I heard someone say once, "Remember, half the people you meet are below average." *(chuckling a little)* Not according to the schools. According to them we're almost all above average. It says so, right there on the report card.

No one is average.

Broaden the spotlight as the angels step back into the light.

NATAL   No one is average. She's right about that much.

ADEK   But not in the right way. She doesn't have any idea what it really means, how true it is. What she's really saying . . .

[Six-minute mark]

NATAL   Because she forgot?

ADEK   That's right.

The angels stay closer to MIKA from here to the end of the drama; use the same lighting for all of them.

[This is the end of the optional section.]

MIKA   *(takes scissors out of the purse)* I thought about using these . . . You're supposed to go along the vein. That's what I heard once—or maybe I saw it in a movie—otherwise it's too easy for 'em to stop the bleeding.

NATAL   No! She's even thought of that?

ADEK   I've tried to stop her—*(tries to take the scissors away from her, they drop to the floor)*

MIKA   *(picks up the scissors, standing up again)* If you don't get it deep enough the first time, they call 'em hesitation marks. They count 'em to tell how many times you tried. To see how serious you were about doing it. Or if you're just doing it to get attention . . .

The pace of this next section is quick, intense, slightly overlapping lines with each other.

NATAL	Take 'em away from her!
MIKA	What does that mean, "do it for attention"?
ADEK	You know I can't! It doesn't work like that!
MIKA	We don't pay attention to the dead, we forget 'em and move on.

[Seven-minute mark]

NATAL	Then what? Do something!
MIKA	We bury 'em and go on with life.
NATAL	*(getting frantic)* She has no idea what she's doing!
MIKA	The people we pay the least amount of attention to are the dead . . .
ADEK	Wait, I have an idea! *(exit, running offstage left)*
MIKA	We're just scratching at the door, trying to get out. But it's closed. I don't know what to do. It doesn't matter. It's closed. They're all closed. *(looks around and then gazes down at the scissors)*

Enter MRS. BINGHAM from stage left.

MRS. BINGHAM	Mika, dear? Is that you?
MIKA	Mrs. Bingham?
MRS. BINGHAM	Are you OK, dear? . . . Mika, are you OK? You look rather upset.
MIKA	I . . . I, um . . . you know my name?
MRS. BINGHAM	Of course I do, sweetie. Oh, careful with those scissors, dear. They look sharp.
MIKA	They are . . . *(hides the scissors in her purse.)* Um, where's your dog?
MRS. BINGHAM	Oh, he's in the yard, running free. He loves it there.
MIKA	Behind the gate?

[Eight-minute mark]

MRS. BINGHAM	Oh, yes. That's where he doesn't need a leash. That's where he can choose where he wants to run. He's free there, dear.
MIKA	I always thought he was trying to get out.
MRS. BINGHAM	*(laughing slightly)* Oh, no. He's just telling you how happy he is to be free. He used to be a stray. Until I gave him a home. C'mon, I'll let you meet him, Mika. *(thoughtfully)* Oh, such a pretty name.

MIKA   My name? Mika?

MRS. BINGHAM Why yes, dearie. You know what it means, don't you?

MIKA   What it means? No. What *does* it mean?

MRS. BINGHAM Why, "God's child," dearie. Your name means "child of God."

MRS. BINGHAM takes MIKA's hand and they exit, stage left.

NATAL   How easily they forget. I'll never understand how easily they forget. *(sits on the apartment steps, shakes his head, and stares at them as the lights fade out.)*

4

BEING HUMAN

God has made everything beautiful for its own time. He has planted eternity in the human heart, but even so, people cannot see the whole scope of God's work from beginning to end.

ECCLESIASTES 3:11

What makes us human? What traits and characteristics do we have in common? Why do we feel so fragmented and alone when we're really so similar to each other? Five people explore what it means to be human in this stream-of-consciousness interpretive reading. At times their confessions are funny; at other times they're unnerving. Use this thought-provoking drama to encourage reflection on life, longing and the realities of being human.

Time: 4 to 5 minutes

Cast

JOE, IRENE, MONICA, AARON, KYLE

Costumes: either casual (such as contemporary clothes) that are representative of your listeners—khakis, jeans, dresses—or neutral, matching clothes, such as black turtle necks and blue jeans

Technical needs: Dim, ambient stage lighting. If desired, have five tight spots on the narrators. Five lapel or headset microphones.

Tips: You might have the actors and actresses remain stationary while reciting their parts, or you might weave the blocking in a tapestry of movement coordinating their placement on stage with their speaking parts. If you choose to use movement, don't let it become too distracting.

Pay special attention to the pace and pauses of this sketch. Let the words sink in. Don't rush it too much.

■ ■ ■

Here are the suggested beginning placements of your actors: MONICA, downstage right; KYLE, upstage just right of center; AARON, downstage center; IRENE, upstage just left of center; JOE, downstage left. All of the actors are on stage as the lights come up and the scene opens.

JOE	I am your next door neighbor.
IRENE	I am your best friend's sister.
AARON	I am your long lost uncle.
KYLE	I am your boss's barber.

After a brief pause

MONICA	I am depressed.
IRENE	I am lonely.
JOE	I am hurting.
AARON	I am ashamed.
KYLE	I am amused.
JOE	I am amazed.
MONICA	I am human.
KYLE	I am changing—
IRENE	Maturing—
JOE	Growing—
MONICA	Becoming—
AARON	I am alive.

After a brief pause

JOE	I am your kid's soccer coach.
IRENE	I had an affair.

After a brief pause

KYLE	I was in a hit-and-run accident and never told anybody.
MONICA	I was your first grade teacher.
IRENE	I sold you that movie ticket last weekend.
KYLE	You've seen me.
JOE	You've looked at me—
MONICA	Looked past me—
AARON	Bumped into me at the ball game—
IRENE	Flipped me off for passing you on the highway.

[One-minute mark]

After a brief pause

JOE	I do drugs.
AARON	I do speed.
KYLE	I drink.
MONICA	I smoke.
IRENE	I eat lots and lots of Twinkies.

After a brief pause

JOE	I lie.
AARON	I steal.
MONICA	I hide.
KYLE	Can you find me?
MONICA	Are you looking?
AARON	Do you know who I am?
IRENE	I look just like you.
·JOE	I am just like you.

After a brief pause

KYLE	I'm lost.
AARON	I'm found.
IRENE	I'm listening.
JOE	I'm searching—
MONICA	Hoping—
KYLE	Dreaming—
MONICA	Believing—
IRENE	Hurrying—
KYLE	On my way to somewhere—
JOE	On my way to something—
IRENE	But, I can't quite remember what it was—
MONICA	Or why I'm going there at all.

After a brief pause

AARON	Sometimes I cope pretty well.
JOE	Sometimes I just give up.

After a brief pause

KYLE	I burp.
JOE	I gargle.
AARON	I dance.
IRENE	I kiss.
MONICA	I cry.
AARON	I yodel.

After a brief pause

JOE	I bleed.

After a brief pause

MONICA	I am in school.
KYLE	I am in prison.
AARON	I am in love.
IRENE	I am in debt up to my eyebrows.

[Two-minute mark]

After a brief pause

JOE	I watch my carbs.
MONICA	I watch my fat.
AARON	I watch the Cubs. *(or insert another popular sports team)*
KYLE	I'm ticklish.
IRENE	I'm hungry.
AARON	I like to go skinny dipping in the moonlight.
JOE	I laugh.
IRENE	I vent.
KYLE	I forgive—
MONICA	But even though I try to, I don't always forget.
IRENE	I have issues.
JOE	I hope.
MONICA	I dream.
AARON	I wonder.
KYLE	I question.
IRENE	I am alive.

After a brief pause

MONICA	I painted my toenails red on Monday night.

AARON	I drive a motorcycle to work.
IRENE	I got a speeding ticket last week.
KYLE	I wear flip-flops.
JOE	I eat oatmeal.
MONICA	I drink half-decaf, extra-hot, tall vanilla lattes with three packs of sugar.

EVERYONE ELSE *(in unison, looking at MONICA)* Huh! So do I!

[Three-minute mark]

After a brief pause

KYLE	I wiggle my toes in the sand.
IRENE	I have pierced ears—
JOE	A pierced tongue—
MONICA	A pierced nose—
KYLE	A pierced heart.
IRENE	Sometimes I feel like crying but mostly I don't.
MONICA	I stuff my feelings.
AARON	I tell people I'm fine, even when I'm not.
JOE	Sometimes I feel like I'm gonna explode.

After a brief pause

MONICA	I am a silent fish, swimming into the depths of myself, descending into the black and inky waters that make me who I am.
KYLE	I am the grip of a rock climber scaling the future. Above me lies the summit, and behind me stretches the emptiness of my past.
IRENE	I am the sail of a small boat in a shallow harbor as the wind fills me and nudges me into the open water and the waiting sea.
AARON	Sometimes I am a shattered mirror.
MONICA	Sometimes I am a dream come true.

[Four-minute mark]

JOE	Who am I?
AARON	What am I doing here?
IRENE	Is there anyone else like me?
MONICA	*Does* anyone else like me?

KYLE   I am alive—

JOE   For now.

After a brief pause

IRENE   Can you find me?

JOE   Are you looking?

AARON   Do you know who I am? *(turns his back to the audience and freezes)*

KYLE   I look just like you. *(turns his back to the audience and freezes)*

MONICA   I am just like you. *(turns her back to the audience and freezes)*

IRENE   I'm a human being . . . being human. *(turns her back to the audience and freezes)*

JOE   As I try to figure out who I am.

Freeze. Fade out. Transition to worship music.

PART TWO

BEHAVIOR

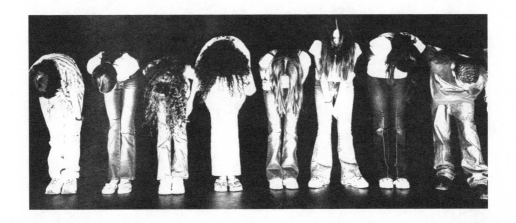

5

CRAVINGS

Temptation comes from the lure of our own evil desires. These evil desires lead to evil actions, and evil actions lead to death.

JAMES 1:14-15

In this contemporary retelling of the folktale of Rapunzel, five characters share their unique perspective on cravings, longings, desire and temptation. During the progression of interwoven monologues, the audience will discover what they crave most and the subtleties of temptation in their own lives.

Time: 4 to 5 minutes

Cast

DAD   (early to mid-forties), a conciliatory guy who doesn't want trouble

MOM   (early to mid-forties), a woman who craves a certain kind of food

RAPUNZEL (late teens to early twenties), Mom and Dad's daughter who just wants to be free

WITCH   (female, early to mid-forties), the neighbor who wants a child of her own

PRINCE   (late teens to early twenties), a guy who wants a girlfriend

Props/set: dark sunglasses for the prince

Technical needs: general stage lighting and five lapel or headset microphones

Tips: While this sketch is written for five actors, with a simple costume piece you could use three actors; one to play the Witch, one to play the part of the Dad and the Prince, one to play the part of Rapunzel and the Mom. Use the costume change to designate which person is addressing the audience and turn with your back to the audience when you're not speaking.

Be sure that all of the cast members come across sympathetically. The Witch is normal, don't talk in a stereotypical "witchy" voice.

This retelling of Rapunzel is pretty close to the original. It's not the watered-down Disney version. Be aware of that when you present it. Because of the graphic nature of certain portions of this sketch, use discernment when performing this drama with young children present.

■ ■ ■

Position the five actors on stage, frozen, with DAD and MOM next to each other, RAPUNZEL and the PRINCE next to each other, and the WITCH in the center. They don't need to be standing in a straight line.

DAD	It all happened back when we were expecting our first child. My wife was about three months pregnant when she started getting these . . . well, cravings.
MOM	For some women it's pickles and ice cream. Only for me it was different.
DAD	She wanted cabbage, of all things. Cabbage. Who knows why.
MOM	*(smiling, shrugging)* I like cabbage.
DAD	Well, anyway, our neighbor had this cabbage patch, right? And she wasn't the most friendly lady in the world, so I figured I'd just slip over and, you know, grab some portable salad after she'd gone to bed.
WITCH	I caught him red-handed trying to steal some of the vegetables from my garden! It was a leafy plant I was growing for the county fair. Looks like cabbage, but it's different. There's a special name for it—it's called Rapunzel.
DAD	She tells me, sure, I could have the Rapunzel stuff, right? But that if I take it, she wants to adopt our baby.

[One-minute mark]

MOM	*(confidentially)* They'd tried to have kids for years, but couldn't. It ended up costing 'em their marriage.
WITCH	All I wanted was a child of my own. "Sure. Whatever. No problem," he says. He couldn't have really cared that much about his baby—
DAD	I was embarrassed, you know. I just wanted to get out of there. So I agreed. I didn't really think anything of it at the time.
MOM	So then, when our daughter was born, *(sarcastically)* Mrs. Cabbage Grower shows up with her lawyer.

DAD	And we didn't have the money to fight it. We hardly had enough to take care of just the two of us. So . . .
MOM	So we handed her over. All because of my cravings. For a stupid little vegetable called—
RAPUNZEL	Rapunzel. I'm called Rapunzel.
WITCH	I raised her as my own daughter—never even told her she was adopted.

[Two-minute mark]

RAPUNZEL	My mom never let me go out much. Drove me crazy. Our house felt like a prison. I'd just sit and stare out the window. Sometimes I'd sing. All I wanted was to be free.
PRINCE	I heard her singing. Her voice was amazing. I had to see her.
WITCH	I tried to stop her. To make her quit. But she wouldn't listen to me. I think she sang just to annoy me—out of spite.
PRINCE	I'd never heard a voice so beautiful.
RAPUNZEL	But he didn't come to take me away. He came for something else. And after a while, I gave him what he wanted, I thought maybe it would help . . . but it didn't.
PRINCE	I visited her every afternoon. I mean, I wanted what any guy wants. A little adventure. A little excitement . . . A little action.
RAPUNZEL	Then one day, she caught us together. In bed. She went crazy, shoved him toward the window just after he'd pulled his jeans on. He stumbled backward and fell off the balcony.

[Three-minute mark]

PRINCE	I landed in the thorns. Face first. The last thing I ever saw were the thorns rushing toward my eyes.
WITCH	I sent Rapunzel away, far away, to boarding school. And I was lonely once again. Just like I'd been at the beginning.
RAPUNZEL	And about three months later, I found out I was pregnant. And I started getting these cravings . . .

Overlap the next few lines so that as one person is beginning to say the word "wanted" the next person is starting his or her lines.

DAD	All I wanted—
MOM	All I wanted—
WITCH	All I wanted—
PRINCE	All I wanted—

RAPUNZEL	All I wanted—
DAD	Was a little peace and quiet.
MOM	Something to eat.
WITCH	A child of my own.
PRINCE	To hook up with someone.
RAPUNZEL	To be free. *(after a pause)* But all I got instead—
DAD	Was hurt.
MOM	Disappointed.
WITCH	Lonely.
PRINCE	Blind.
RAPUNZEL	Pregnant.
MOM	All I wanted—
DAD	Was something,
PRINCE	Anything—
WITCH	To satisfy my cravings.
RAPUNZEL	What's wrong with that?
PRINCE	Why can't I have what I want out of life?
MOM	It's not fair.

[Four-minute mark]

DAD	In the end, I wasn't satisfied. I was never satisfied.
PRINCE	I was just filled with more cravings. For something else.
MOM	Why is it so hard to be satisfied?
RAPUNZEL	Maybe because, deep down, what I really want, more than anything else, is to live happily ever after.
DAD	I just don't know where to look to find it.

Freeze. Fade out.

6

VIRGO

And so, dear Christian friends, I plead with you to give your bodies to God. Let them be a living and holy sacrifice—the kind he will accept.

When you think of what he has done for you, is this too much to ask?

Don't copy the behavior and customs of this world, but let God transform you into a new person by changing the way you think.

Then you will know what God wants you to do, and you will know how good and pleasing and perfect his will really is.

ROMANS 12:1-2

Steve and Laura are on a quiet weekend getaway. When Steve starts coming on to Laura, she confronts him about the way he's been treating her. By highlighting sexual choices and relationships, this honest drama explores convictions, why we have them and how we sometimes follow the letter but not the spirit of the law.

Time: 6 to 7 minutes

Cast

STEVE   a twenty-three-year-old guy who thinks it's wrong to have sex outside of marriage but has pushed the boundaries as far as he can with his girlfriend

LAURA   a twenty-one-year-old woman who is hurt and confused with the mixed signals she's getting from Steve. She thinks she must have done something to turn him off since he doesn't seem to want to sleep with her.

Costumes: Jeans, t-shirts and flip-flops or other cool hang-out clothes. Steve is wearing a baseball cap (see end of drama). He and Laura are on a romantic walk on the beach near her uncle's cabin.

Props/set: a CD of ambient beach sounds (if desired); perhaps a picnic table or dock for them to sit on

Technical needs: general stage lighting and two lapel or headset microphones

Tips: Really let your actors step into their parts. Be sure to talk with them about the intimate nature of this drama and make sure they're comfortable in their roles.

As this drama progresses, Laura moves from being confused to being frustrated. Steve is always coming on to her but then pulling back before they have sex. She feels hurt and lonely since all the other guys she has dated have been a lot more interested in sleeping with her.

Because of the graphic nature of certain portions of this sketch, use discernment when performing this drama with young children present.

■ ■ ■

It's night time at a quiet, private lakeshore north of the city. STEVE and LAURA are walking hand in hand along the beach, looking up at the stars. He's being flirty, and she is a bit cool to his advances. She has something big on her mind that's distracting her.

STEVE	*(totally coming on to her)* It's a beautiful night, isn't it, Laura.
LAURA	It sure is.
STEVE	Quiet.
LAURA	Yeah.
STEVE	Kinda romantic.
LAURA	Yeah.
STEVE	*(gazing at the stars)* You know any constellations?
LAURA	The only one I can ever find is the Big Dipper.
STEVE	Yeah, me too, and the North Star. That's all I really remember. I used to be into constellations when I was kid.
LAURA	Really?
STEVE	Yeah. I could find like twenty or thirty of 'em—Cassiopeia, Scorpio, Virgo . . . Some people say our futures are determined by the stars.
LAURA	I don't think they are. I think the future's up to us.
STEVE	Hmm. Who knows. *(looking around)* The stars out here are amazing!

If staging and view lines allow, they could sit on the sand facing the audience to watch the waves come in, or sit on a picnic table or dock if desired.

LAURA   Yeah, my uncle lets me come up here pretty much whenever I want to. Get away from the city and all. You know. Relax.

STEVE   *(snuggling close)* It is relaxing, isn't it?

LAURA   *(pulling away a little)* Yeah, he has the only cabin on this side of the lake.

[One-minute mark]

STEVE   *(after a pause)* So, what did you want to tell me, Laura? What's the big surprise?

LAURA   *(awkwardly)* Oh, I don't know. I just . . . Well, we've been seeing each other for a while, right?

This section of her leading up to the question should be pretty smooth and quick, don't draw it out too long.

STEVE   Yeah.

LAURA   We get along pretty well, don't we?

STEVE   Of course.

LAURA   We have fun together.

STEVE   Uh-huh.

LAURA   And I don't know about you, but I think you're pretty awesome.

STEVE   Well, you're right . . . I mean, I think you are too.

LAURA   I'm not really sure how to say this . . . Um, OK. So, here goes—

STEVE   Don't be nervous, Laura. It's OK.

LAURA   Right. OK. Steve, we've been going out for, like, four months—

STEVE   Uh-huh?—

LAURA   And, um . . .

STEVE   What is it?

LAURA   *(quickly)* What is it about me you don't like?

STEVE   What do you mean? I like everything about you.

LAURA   But you don't love me, though, do you?

STEVE   Of course. Yeah. I love you. What's going on?

LAURA   All we ever do is make out.

STEVE   We talk and stuff.

LAURA   Yeah, but . . .

STEVE   But what?

[Two-minute mark]

LAURA   *(after a pause)* But all this time we haven't slept together. Every time I think we're gonna go all the way, you pull back. Get distant. I don't get it. Aren't you attracted to me?

STEVE   Yeah, I am. I just—

LAURA   What? Did I do something? Say something?

STEVE   No, you've been great!

LAURA   Then what?

STEVE   I just . . . I don't feel right about it.

LAURA   You're not gay are you?

STEVE   No, of course not.

LAURA   Are you seeing someone else?

STEVE   No!

LAURA   It's me, then. It's something about me.

STEVE   No, it's not you.

LAURA   How could it not be me? I don't get it. Most guys I've gone out with, well, let's just say, they seem a lot more interested in me than you do.

STEVE   I *am* interested in you.

LAURA   Then what?

STEVE   I am interested, it's just *(sighing)* . . . ever since I was a kid I always thought you were supposed to wait, you know, save yourself for marriage.

LAURA   Save yourself?

[Three-minute mark]

STEVE   Yeah. My mom always told me sex was a gift that you give to your spouse. And that we shouldn't go around unwrapping other people's presents.

LAURA   Your *mom* told you?

STEVE   Well, yeah.

LAURA   Steve, you're a big boy now. You don't have to do what your mom says anymore. You can make your own choices.

STEVE   I know.

LAURA   *(after a pause)* So you've never—?

STEVE	No.
LAURA	C'mon, really?
STEVE	Yeah, really.
LAURA	Never?
STEVE	Not yet. No.
LAURA	Whoa.
STEVE	C'mon, we've talked about this before. I grew up going to a church where they taught that you're supposed to wait.
LAURA	So it's some kind of religious thing, then?
STEVE	Maybe. I mean, I guess so.
LAURA	But, Steve, if we care about each other, if we love each other, why wouldn't God want us to be happy?
STEVE	He does, I mean. Of course he wants us to be happy.
LAURA	But I'm not happy.
STEVE	(hurt) You're not?
LAURA	No, I mean, I'm happy being with you, but there's more to a relationship than good times and making out and holding hands—
STEVE	Well, there's more to a relationship than sex.

[Four-minute mark]

LAURA	(a bit sarcastically) I never thought I'd hear a guy say that!
STEVE	C'mon, cut it out. This is serious.
LAURA	I know it is! That's my point. It is serious. (getting upset) So, what is it? What do you want? Every night it's the kisses and the whispers and the hugs and the flirting and the teasing. Every night!
STEVE	I care about you. I . . . I love you, Laura.
LAURA	(coldly) You love me. Oh, really? Look, I respect your convictions or your religion or whatever, it's just that . . . well . . . I'm not sure how long I can keep this up.
STEVE	What do you mean? Keep what up?
LAURA	Keep this up! Us! Us! We're here on a romantic beach on a quiet, private weekend together. We care about each other, and all you can talk about are some religious laws your mom taught you when you were a kid!
STEVE	(getting confused) You're twisting what I said around, I—

[Five-minute mark]

LAURA   *(interrupting)* Look, Steve. I like you. I do. And I'm trying to understand, but, well, I'm confused. You're giving me mixed signals. You tell me how much you love me, you hold me, you tease me . . . you touch me . . . *(pause, let that line sink in)* but you won't go all the way. It hurts.

STEVE   I thought you liked it when I touch you. I thought—

LAURA   Steve! I don't know what's going on anymore . . . *(after a pause)* It's like you're using me . . . I just don't think I'm getting what I need out of this relationship.

STEVE   Love isn't supposed to be about what you get out of a relationship. It's supposed to be about what you put into it.

LAURA   So why don't you put something into it, huh? If you really care about me, give me something. C'mon! Don't just take from me all the time! Toying with me, playing with my emotions, leading me on and then pulling away. You won't take it to the next level.

STEVE   *(more confusion)* It's, it's not the same thing.

LAURA   Yes it is! Look, I'm getting cold . . . I think I'm gonna head inside.

[Six-minute mark]

STEVE   No, Laura. Come back, please. Laura! I . . . I want to . . . I do.

LAURA   You do?

STEVE   Of course I want to . . . It's just . . . I don't know if I should.

LAURA   *(coldly)* Oh. I see. You don't know if you should. Look, if you don't want to be with me, fine, just say so. I'm going inside. *(exit stage left)*

STEVE   *(to LAURA)* But I do want to be with you! I . . . I . . . *(to himself)* I just don't know what to do. I just don't know what to do. *(gets mad, throws his baseball cap on the ground or pounds the ground and puts his face in his hands as the lights fade out.)*

7

LOVE THY NEIGHBOR

The King will reply, "I tell you the truth, whatever you did for one of the least of these brothers of mine, you did for me."

MATTHEW 25:40 NIV

Lawrence is trying to study his Bible when he's interrupted by a curious and annoying young man. As Lawrence loses his patience and decides he's finally had enough, he discovers something shocking about his new friend. Use this sketch to get people thinking about compassion, living out their faith and understanding what lies at the heart of the Christian story.

Time: 4 to 5 minutes

Cast

LAWRENCE   an uptight, impatient guy who's trying to study his Bible

BLADE   a twenty-something, outgoing, postmodern guy who just wants to carry on a friendly conversation

Props/set: a large bag of sour cream and onion rippled potato chips, a large Bible (the verse quoted in the text is from the New International Version), a park bench, a portable CD player and headphones, breadcrumbs (optional)

Technical needs: general stage lighting or a single tight spot and two cordless lapel or headset microphones. Type the text for Mathew 25:40 NIV onto your video or media program and project it on the screen after the drama has finished and before the speaker comes up on stage.

Tips: The kicker is that Blade is really Jesus in disguise. Jesus made it clear that when we show practical compassion and love for others, we are doing it for him. We love God by loving other people with the love of Jesus. It's not always (or even often) comfortable or convenient, but it is essential.

If desired, Blade could be breaking off breadcrumbs and tossing them to imaginary ducks.

∎ ∎ ∎

LAWRENCE is seated on a park bench when the lights come up and BLADE enters. BLADE has his portable CD player or iPod and is jamming to the music. LAWRENCE tries to read for a few minutes, finally finds the music too distracting and decides to ask BLADE to turn it down.

LAWRENCE   Um, could you turn that down? Please?

BLADE   Huh?

LAWRENCE   Could you turn that down! Turn the music down. I'm trying to read here.

BLADE   Oh, sure, no problem. *(turns off the headphones, opens up the bag of chips and begins munching really loudly. This goes on for a bit.)*

LAWRENCE   Um, do you mind?

BLADE   Huh?

LAWRENCE   I said, do you mind?!

BLADE   Oh, no. Go ahead. *(offers him the bag of chips)*

LAWRENCE   No, listen, I don't want your chips. I'm trying to concentrate.

BLADE   Uh-huh.

LAWRENCE   I'm trying to read this book.

BLADE   Yeah?

LAWRENCE   Right. And your chips, all that crunching and munching—

BLADE   They're good.

LAWRENCE   I'm sure they are.

BLADE   Sour cream and onion.

LAWRENCE   Very nice.

BLADE   Rippled too.

LAWRENCE   Yes, yes, I see. But the thing is, all that crunching and munching is distracting me. Makes it hard to read.

[One-minute mark]

BLADE   Oh.

LAWRENCE   So, if you don't mind.

BLADE   Oh. OK, sure. *(puts the chips away)*

LAWRENCE   Thank you.

BLADE   *(after a pause, looking over LAWRENCE'S shoulder)* So, whatcha readin'?

LAWRENCE	I'm sorry?
BLADE	Whatcha readin' there?
LAWRENCE	It's . . . it's a Bible. See?
BLADE	Oh, yeah, the Holy Bible.
LAWRENCE	Right. The Holy Bible.
BLADE	Yeah . . . I've heard of that one before.
LAWRENCE	I should hope so.
BLADE	So . . . is it any good?
LAWRENCE	Of course it's good. It's very good. It's the Bible!
BLADE	Oh. Right, yeah. OK.
LAWRENCE	The Bible. The Holy Bible.
BLADE	OK. *(looks over his shoulder again. After a pause)* Is it as good as the *Lord of the Rings* books? I really like those.
LAWRENCE	Listen, I'm trying to focus here, OK?
BLADE	OK, sure . . . sure . . . *(after a pause)* So?

[Two-minute mark]

LAWRENCE	What!
BLADE	So, is it as good?
LAWRENCE	Yes, it's as good! It's better than the *Lord of the Rings,* OK? It's better than anything! It's the Bible—all right?
BLADE	Yeah. Sure. Good. The Bible.
LAWRENCE	That's right. The Bible.
BLADE	*(pause)* So what's it about?
LAWRENCE	What's it abou . . . ? Listen—it's the Bible!
BLADE	*(expectantly)* OK? . . .
LAWRENCE	It's about God and everything like that.
BLADE	Uh-huh.
LAWRENCE	Jesus and stuff. You know.
BLADE	OK.
LAWRENCE	I'm reading all about him in the New Testament.
BLADE	So it's good, then, huh? The New Testament?
LAWRENCE	Haven't you ever read the Bible?
BLADE	Well, not the whole thing, no. Not the New Testament part.

LAWRENCE	*(suddenly feeling evangelistic, offers Bible)* Do you want to?
BLADE	*(looking over the Bible)* Um, I don't know. It's a pretty big book. Really thick. What's the plot?
LAWRENCE	The plot?
BLADE	Yeah, you know. What happens? Like in the *Lord of the Rings,* Gandalf battling that shadow-and-flame demon-thing. You know, the action and stuff. The plot.

[Three-minute mark]

LAWRENCE	Oh, um. Well, it's about God.
BLADE	OK.
LAWRENCE	And Jesus.
BLADE	Uh-huh.
LAWRENCE	And stuff.
BLADE	Right. So you said.
LAWRENCE	Yeah.
BLADE	*(hands the Bible back to LAWRENCE)* So you're not too far into it, huh? What, did you just pick up a copy?
LAWRENCE	No, I've had it for a long time! My whole life! I read it all the time! It's the Holy Bible!
BLADE	You read it all the time?
LAWRENCE	Yes! Of course!
BLADE	So you know what it's all about?
LAWRENCE	Yes, I do! Of course!
BLADE	God?
LAWRENCE	Right.
BLADE	And Jesus?
LAWRENCE	Yes.
BLADE	And stuff?
LAWRENCE	That's right. Exactly. *And stuff.* Stuff like faith and hope and charity!
BLADE	Charity.
LAWRENCE	*(very impatiently)* Yes. Charity—that means *love.* In fact that's what the Bible is about! Love! Love, joy, peace, patience, OK? Kindness, goodness, gentleness, faithfulness and self-control. Got it? OK? All right? That's the main point!

BLADE   Oh. Love.

LAWRENCE   *(yelling)* Love! That's right. It's the main point. Love is the main point!

BLADE   Oh. *(offers LAWRENCE the bag of chips)* You sure you don't want a chip or something. They're really good. Kinda have a calming effect—

[Four-minute mark]

LAWRENCE   Look, I'm sorry, but it's just too distracting sitting here talking to you. *(gets up to leave)*

BLADE   OK. See ya. Um, what did you say your name is?

LAWRENCE   My name is Lawrence, OK!

BLADE   See ya, Lawrence.

LAWRENCE   Goodbye—um, what did you say your name is?

BLADE   I didn't. But you'll find it right there, on page one thousand fifty nine. Second paragraph, I think. About half-way down.

LAWRENCE   Huh?

BLADE   See ya later, Lawrence. *(stands up and exits munching on some chips)*

LAWRENCE   *(looking in his Bible)* One thousand . . . fifty nine . . . second paragraph . . . "She will give birth to a son, and you are to give him the name Jesus, because he will save his people from their sins." *(see Matthew 1:21 NIV)* Oh, boy.

Freeze. Fade out. As the lights fade and before the speaker comes on stage, project the text for Mathew 25:40: "The King will reply, 'I tell you the truth, whatever you did for one of the least of these brothers of mine, you did for me.'" (NIV) onto the screen.

8

No Trespassing

You have heard that the law of Moses says, "Do not commit adultery." But I say, anyone who even looks at a woman with lust in his eye has already committed adultery with her in his heart.

MATTHEW 5:27-28

Earl is minding his own business when two police officers show up to arrest him. When they explain that they're members of the International Thought Police, he's forced to admit that his thoughts really were trespassing. This lighthearted drama explores the idea of self-control as it relates to not just our bodies but also our thoughts. What does it mean to "take captive every thought" (2 Corinthians 10:5 NIV)? What changes do we need to make in our lives to really start living out that verse?

Time: 6 to 7 minutes

Cast

EARL   (late twenties), an unsuspecting normal guy who ends up trying to justify his less than perfect thought life

OFFICER 11   (male or female), a senior officer of the International Thought Police who is trying to convince Earl that he is a criminal

OFFICER 12   (male), Officer 11's smart-alecky sidekick

Costumes: casual, contemporary clothes for Earl; uniforms for Officers 11 and 12. The officers can wear typical police-officer outfits or have a cloak-and-dagger thing going, with an overcoat and dark shades.

Props/set: a rake, perhaps a pile of leaves (these could be imaginary) a wallet and driver's license for Earl; pens, notebooks, walkie-talkies and uniforms for Officers 11 and 12

Technical needs: general stage lighting and three lapel or headset microphones

Tips: This drama will work best if the characters are a little quirky, almost absurd. Encourage your actors not to play the script too straight but rather over the top. Most of the blocking grows from the two police officers; Earl just remains pretty much in center stage and clueless as the drama progresses.

Feel free to add to this drama personal touches or changes that might work better for your church setting. For example, instead of karate moves, you could have the officer (gently) tackle Earl.

■   ■   ■

EARL's front yard at 4:30 p.m. EARL has just gotten home from work and is raking the lawn before going inside for a bite to eat. He's on stage raking leaves when the lights come up and the scene begins.

EARL	*(humming or whistling, daydreaming)*
OFFICER 11	*(entering from stage left)* Stop right there!
EARL	Huh?
OFFICER 11	Don't move, Mister!
EARL	What's going on?
OFFICER 11	*(into a walkie-talkie)* I think we got him.
OFFICER 12	*(from offstage)* Roger that. *(enter from stage right)*
EARL	What in the . . . ? Who are you guys?
OFFICER 11	No quick moves, buddy.
OFFICER 12	*(doing karate moves all around EARL)* We've got you covered.
OFFICER 11	Now drop the rake and put your hands up.
OFFICER 12	And let's see some I.D.!
EARL	*(reaches into his pocket and pulls out his driver's license)* Is there a problem or something?
OFFICER 11	*(looking over the license)* Hmm . . .
OFFICER 12	It's him.
OFFICER 11	Sure is.
EARL	Listen, fellas, I don't know what's going on, but I haven't done anything wrong.
OFFICER 11	*(giving his wallet back)* I'm afraid you *have* done something wrong, Mr. Beckman. We're gonna have to take you in.

EARL   But what . . . what are you talking about? I was just standing here minding my own business—

OFFICER 12   Aha! You *weren't* minding your own business!

EARL   Yes, yes, I was!

OFFICER 11   I'm afraid you were trespassing, sir.

[One-minute mark]

EARL   Trespassing? What? This is my lawn! I'm raking my yard! That's my house right there! How could I be trespassing? I was here the whole time!

OFFICER 11   Yes, sir, *you* were here the whole time, but I'm afraid your thoughts weren't. It's your *thoughts* that were trespassing.

EARL   My thoughts?

OFFICER 12   That's right.

EARL   How could my thoughts be trespassing?!

OFFICER 11   Going where they're not supposed to go. That's called trespassing.

EARL   Look, what's going on? *(looking around for a camera)* Am I on one of those hidden-camera reality shows or something?

OFFICER 11   No, sir. We're with the International Thought Police.

EARL   Never heard of 'em.

OFFICER 12   We're new.

EARL   Oh.

OFFICER 12   It's all very hush, hush.

EARL   I see.

OFFICER 11   Instead of waiting until crimes occur, we stop 'em before they ever happen. *(taps his head)* And we've been monitoring your thoughts.

EARL   *(skeptically)* My thoughts, huh? You've been monitoring my thoughts? All right then, what am I thinking right now?

[Two-minute mark]

OFFICER 11   That we're a bunch of bozos who better get off your yard before you call the real police.

EARL   *(surprised)* Whoa, you're right . . . What about now?

OFFICER 12   That your friend Gary set us up to come over here to get you back for the whole duct-tape-and-gerbil practical joke you pulled on him last November.

EARL	*(impressed)* Man, you guys are *good*.
OFFICER 12	I knew you were gonna say that.
EARL	Right.
OFFICER 12	That too.
EARL	All right! OK! That's enough! I get it, I get it.
OFFICER 12	I know.
EARL	*(sigh)* But how do you guys do it?
OFFICER 11	*(throughout the drama, whenever the officers say this phrase, they strike a law-enforcement pose together)* We have—
OFFICER 12	The technology.

[Three-minute mark]

EARL	Oh. Great.
OFFICER 11	And you were trespassing on Mr. Saunder's property over there.
EARL	But I was right here the whole time!
OFFICER 12	No, your thoughts. You were thinking about how nice it would be to ride in his new Porsche 911 Carrera, weren't you?
EARL	How did you know that?
OFFICER 11	We have—
OFFICER 12	The technology.
EARL	Well, I mean—
OFFICER 11	That's trespassing. And you were thinking about how nice it would be to have his job too, if I'm not mistaken.
EARL	I'm . . . um . . . Well, he does make pretty good money . . .
OFFICER 12	And his wife, Mr. Beckman? Eh? Shame on you!
EARL	C'mon! How could you know all that!
OFFICER 11	We have—
EARL	I know, I know, the technology.
OFFICER 12	That's right.
OFFICER 11	We've been watching you for some time now. Especially after that affair you had.
EARL	What! I've never had an affair!
OFFICER 12	You thought about having one.
EARL	When!
OFFICER 11	*(flipping open a notebook)* According to my notes here . . . let's see . . .

OFFICER 12	*(pointing, helping him find it)* There.
OFFICER 11	Oh, yes. There it is. Last week when you were at that club downtown and met that cute blonde accountant *(or say "accounting student" if your audience is all college students)*
EARL	That's far enough, Mr. Mind Reader. I get the picture. OK, yeah. I admit it. I thought about it. But I didn't do anything!
OFFICER 11	Have you ever heard the saying "it's the thought that counts"?

[Four-minute mark]

EARL	That's for Mother's Day cards!
OFFICER 12	Which reminds me—
EARL	Oh, yeah. Oops.
OFFICER 12	Forgot again this year, huh?
EARL	Um . . . Yeah.
OFFICER 12	I know.
EARL	Stop that.
OFFICER 11	All right, that's enough, you two.
OFFICER 12	I knew he was gonna say that.
OFFICER 11	I know.
OFFICER 12	Me too.
EARL	Look, you two need professional help.
OFFICERS	*(in unison)* We know.
OFFICER 11	*(flipping open the notebook)* In addition, I have quite a number of other offenses listed here. From theft . . . to murder . . .
EARL	Murder!
OFFICER 12	*(moving in closer)* Time to take you in.
EARL	Look. This isn't right. You've got the wrong guy! I've never murdered anyone!
OFFICER 11	Actually, you did. *(flipping open the notebook).* Last year you were driving through Chicago *(or another nearby city famous for reckless driving)* and that guy in the pick-up kept cutting you off in traffic . . . Remember?
EARL	In Chicago, everyone cuts you off in traffic!
OFFICER 12	I know.
OFFICER 11	*(reading from the notebook)* And you said, quote, "Buddy, I wish you were dead!" End quote.

EARL   I did?

[Five-minute mark]

OFFICER 12   Yup. Wishing someone was dead. It's the thought that counts. Murder.

EARL   But I only *thought* those things!

OFFICER 12   What do you mean, *only* thought them?

EARL   I didn't *do* them!

OFFICER 11   Mr. Beckman, if you did something without thinking about it, would you be responsible? Say, for example, getting into a car accident because you weren't paying attention?

EARL   Well, yeah. Of course!

OFFICER 12   So, why wouldn't you be even *more* guilty for thinking something but not doing it?

EARL   Um . . .

OFFICER 11   What's the difference? You're responsible for what you do without thinking about it; why shouldn't you be held accountable for what you think about but don't do?

EARL   *(confused)* Because . . . I don't know . . . I know there's a good reason, though, I just can't think of it right now.

OFFICER 11   Think about it.

EARL   I am.

OFFICER 12   I know.

OFFICER 11   *(paces as he explains this.)* Look, if you think about murdering someone and then do it, it's premeditated—

OFFICER 12   First degree murder—

OFFICER 11   Right. But if you lose your temper and hit someone and they die, it's considered manslaughter. So if you plan it out, you're more guilty because you *thought* about it.

[Six-minute mark]

OFFICER 12   It's the *thought* that counts.

OFFICER 11   You're just as responsible for what you think as you are for what you do.

EARL   You're pullin' my leg, right?

OFFICER 11   Nope, it's time to go, Mr. Beckman.

OFFICER 12   And no funny business. Remember, I know what you're thinking.

EARL   I know, I know.

OFFICER 12   I knew that.

[Possible ending 1]

OFFICER 11   *(begins leading EARL off stage)*

EARL   *(to OFFICER 12)* I just thought something else about you.

OFFICER 12   I know.

EARL   It wasn't very nice.

OFFICER 12   I know that too.

EARL   Yeah, yeah, you have the technology.

OFFICER 12   I know.

As they exit, fade out the lights.

PART THREE

RELATIONSHIPS

9

WELCOME TO MAG ONE

Therefore confess your sins to each other and pray for each

other so that you may be healed.

JAMES 5:16 NIV

All the guys at the "MAG ONE Men's Accountability Group" are pretty comfortable sharing their problems—or are they? When their new member, Zak, tells about one of his struggles, the truth about the group comes to the surface. This humorous drama reveals some of the ways we typically hide the struggles we have.

Time: 4 to 5 minutes

Cast

BOB   the enthusiastic small group Bible study leader for MAG ONE

TODD   a normal guy

MARCOS   a normal guy

RANDALL   the group member who has brought his friend to visit

ZAK   an honest, authentic and genuine guy who is visiting MAG ONE for the first time

Props/set: four big fat Bibles for the regular group members (minus Zak), a Bible study guide for Bob, bags of chips, salsa, beef jerky and other snacks for the guys (these are hidden behind their chairs and in coat pockets at the beginning of the drama)

Technical needs: general stage lighting or a single tight spot and five cordless lapel or headset microphones

Tips: Whenever the script says MAG GUYS, it is referring to all the members of the group except for Zak.

The Mag Guys have this bit that they repeat throughout the drama. They cheer (or grunt) in unison and yell "Huh!" Think of a football-huddle grunt. Practice this routine so your cast can perform it together when noted in the script.

If you perform this sketch with teen or college students, you may want to call it "GAG ONE: Guy's Accountability Group."

■ ■ ■

As the lights come up and the scene opens, the five guys are seated in a semicircle facing the audience, making small talk. Then BOB addresses the group members and the sketch begins.

BOB	OK, guys! Let's get started! Welcome back to MAG ONE! So, how was everyone's week?
TODD	Good.
MARCOS	Fine.
RANDALL	Good.
BOB	Great! Well, praise God!
TODD	Amen!
MARCOS	Hallelujah!
RANDALL	You said it, brother!
MAG GUYS	*(cheering in unison, as if in a football huddle)* Huh!
BOB	So, and who is this here?
RANDALL	This is my buddy Zak from work. He just got transferred into my division. He's new to the area.
BOB	Hey, Zak, welcome to MAG ONE!
TODD	Men's—
MARCOS	Accountability—
RANDALL	Group!
BOB	*(to ZAK)* That's the MAG part; it's an acronym.
TODD	*(proudly)* I thought it up.
ZAK	Very nice.
BOB	And ONE because we're all one in the Spirit. Right, guys?
TODD	Amen!
MARCOS	Hallelujah!
RANDALL	You said it, brother!
MAG GUYS	*(cheering in unison)* Huh!
ZAK	Thanks, guys. It's, uh . . . it's good to be here.
BOB	Here there are no secrets, Zak, and everything that's said here—
RANDALL, MARCOS and TODD	*(in unison)* Stays here!

MAG GUYS	*(cheering in unison)* Huh!
BOB	Right!
ZAK	Wow, well, great! This is just what I've been looking for.

[One-minute mark]

BOB	Well, let's take a moment to introduce ourselves to our new member!

Make these exchanges quick and friendly.

MARCOS	Hi, Zak, I'm Marcos.
ZAK	Good to meet you.
TODD	Todd—I'm the one who thought up the acronym.
ZAK	Right.
RANDALL	You already know me, Randall.
BOB	And I'm Bob.
ZAK	OK, well it's great to meet you guys.
MAG GUYS	*(nod and agree, "yeah, you, too . . .", etc.)*
BOB	Now, let's see . . . what were we gonna talk about this week? *(all the guys except for ZAK open up their Bibles in unison.)* Um, sexual purity. *(MAG GUYS all nod and look nervous.)* Yeah, sexual purity. That's right. So . . . any of you guys have any struggles this week in the, um, in the area of sexual purity?
TODD	Nope.
MARCOS	Not me.
RANDALL	Not really. Nope.
BOB	*(relieved)* Great! Well, praise God!
TODD	Amen!
MARCOS	Halleluiah!
RANDALL	*(thankfully)* You said it, brother!
MAG GUYS	*(cheering in unison)* Huh!
BOB	OK, then! *(looking in the Bible study booklet)* Let's see, what's next on the old agenda—
ZAK	Um, I did.

Awkward silence; everyone looks at ZAK.

BOB	Huh? What was that, Zak?
ZAK	I said, "I did." Last night. I had a bit of a struggle. I, um, watched the Miss Universe pageant . . . Did you guys see it?

[Two-minute mark]

Each excuse is awkward as the group members make them up.

TODD   Um . . . no, I was reading my . . . um, my Bible.

MARCOS   Uh, I was . . . witnessing to my . . . my mother-in-law.

RANDALL Praying. I was busy praying and fasting last night. Yeah.

ZAK   Oh, well, then you missed it, I guess . . . Anyway, the women were gorgeous. Mainly, it was Miss Australia that did it for me. I . . . um . . . well, I lusted after her. I admit it. I'm really ashamed, but when I saw her walk on stage, I just couldn't help it—

TODD   Oh, no kidding. I mean she was hot. With that sparkly red bikini . . . whoa . . .

ZAK   I thought you didn't see it.

TODD   Um, well. I was flipping channels looking for the, uh . . . the Franklin Graham special . . .

ZAK   Oh.

TODD   He's preaching a crusade in Ecuador—

ZAK   I see.

TODD   I was watching that—

ZAK   Uh-huh.

TODD   Yup.

ZAK   Well . . . I, um, I need your help, guys. 'Cause I didn't change the channel. I didn't look away. And then when Miss Trinidad walked on stage in that evening gown to sing that solo from—

[Three-minute mark]

MARCOS   *La Traviata.* Oh, it almost brought me to tears.

ZAK   So you saw it too?

MARCOS   Um, I heard about it. This morning. On *Focus on the Family.*

BOB   They covered the Miss Universe Pageant?

MARCOS   A brief little segment there.

ZAK   Oh. Well, now today, it's been really tough. I mean, I can't get some of those women out of my head. Like Miss Jamaica . . . Miss Ukraine . . .

BOB   Miss Switzerland . . . Miss Venezuela . . . Miss Puerto Rico . . .

ZAK   You saw it too, Bob?

BOB   Um, my, my wife was watching it. I just saw a little bit as I was walking through the living room . . . to get my checkbook . . . to write my tithes and offerings.

ZAK   I see.

RANDALL   And then, when they did that background piece on Miss Canada going to modeling school . . . Oh! I almost choked on my popcorn!

ZAK   I thought you were fasting?

RANDALL   *(awkwardly)* I was. In between kernels.

ZAK   Oh. So all you guys saw it then?

MAG GUYS   *(nod guiltily)*

[Four-minute mark]

ZAK   Well, why didn't you say something at the beginning of the meeting?

String their mumbled apologies together, overlapping them.

BOB   Sorry.

TODD   Yeah, blew it there.

MARCOS   I should have said something—

RANDALL   Just a little embarrassed you know . . .

ZAK   Look, maybe this group isn't what I was looking for after all. I really need a bunch of guys I can be honest with about my struggles and stuff. See you at work, Randall. *(exit)*

MAG GUYS   *(watch him leave)*

BOB   *(after a pause)* Well, um, did any of you guys have any other struggles this week?

TODD   Nope.

MARCOS   Not me.

RANDALL   Not really. Nope.

BOB   Great! Well, praise God!

TODD   Amen!

MARCOS   Hallelujah!

RANDALL   You said it brother!

BOB   All right, so if there's no other problems—

RANDALL   *(reverently)* Wait a minute, guys. I think maybe we should pray for Zak.

TODD   *(reverently)* Yeah.

MARCOS   *(reverently)* Good idea.

BOB   *(reverently)* Right.

RANDALL   Right after snacks!

MAG GUYS   All right! *(cheering in unison)* Huh!

Pull out the bags of chips and salsa, beef jerky, etc. from behind their chairs and begin to eat as the lights fade out.

10

THE PHONE CALL

You know the guidelines we laid out for you from the Master Jesus. God wants you to live a pure life. Keep yourselves from sexual promiscuity.

1 THESSALONIANS 4:2-3 *THE MESSAGE*

Often we are quick to justify the "little" steps we take toward disobedience. When Jesus whispers to our hearts, do we listen to him or turn up the volume of our own desires? In this scene Liz is being tempted to have an affair with a guy she recently met. The phone is ringing and she thinks she knows who it is—her new friend. As she tries to decide what to do, we hear another perspective on her problem. But who will she listen to? Will she answer the phone or not?

Time: 4 minutes

Cast

LIZ a twenty-seven-year-old woman who is having a rough time in her marriage and is being drawn toward another man

JOSH a thirty-three-year-old guy who genuinely cares for Liz and wants what's best for her

Props/set: two chairs, two lamps and two end tables (don't use a matching set); two cordless phones (not necessarily cell phones), a framed photograph of the actress and her husband (or boyfriend), a laptop computer

Technical needs: General stage lighting or two spots (one focused on the chair on stage left and one on the chair on stage right) and two cordless lapel or headset microphones. During this sketch, a phone rings on stage. You may want to record the phone ringing and burn it into a CD so you can control the volume of the rings at the end of the sketch, or have someone call the phone.

Tips: The actors are not addressing each other in this sketch, but are talking to the audience. (Josh does address Liz toward the end of the sketch, but she remains oblivious to him.) Josh is really the voice of Jesus, but the audience doesn't realize that until the end of the sketch.

Liz should reveal her uneasiness and nervousness by her actions and by the way she dusts the end table or types on the laptop. Either way, she shouldn't pretend to type or pretend to dust—she should really do it.

Don't feel like you need to keep Liz and Josh seated. They can stand and walk around their chairs and so forth as long as they don't directly address each other until the moment when Josh begins to talk to Liz.

■ ■ ■

LIZ is at home. It's 11:07 a.m. on Tuesday morning. An end table with a chair, lamp, phone and framed picture lie on stage left. On stage right is a different style chair and lamp. JOSH is seated there in the dark. A phone is on his end table as well. Bring up the light on LIZ.

When the lights come up, LIZ is dusting her lamp or typing on her laptop. Then, when her phone rings she doesn't answer it, just stares at it. The phone rings seven or eight times, long enough to make everyone in the audience uncomfortable. Still, she doesn't answer it. Finally, it stops ringing and she turns to the audience and addresses them.

LIZ   (warmly) I met him last month at Starbucks. I mean we just talked, that's all . . . I saw he was reading his Bible and I was, like, "Hey, look, I brought mine too!" I was just trying to be polite.

And we got to talking. He's in advertising. Only moved to the area a year or so ago . . . He told me how he and his wife were going through a tough time, and I mentioned how Greg and I hadn't really been connecting too well lately either. And, well . . . it was just good to have someone to talk to.

[One-minute mark]

(after a pause) I only gave him my number so he could get in touch with me if he ever needed someone to talk to or vent with or whatever . . . I didn't do anything wrong. (freeze)

As she finishes, bring up the spotlight on Josh.

JOSH   I've been trying to get through to her for a while. But it's like she doesn't want to talk to me anymore. I don't understand. We really seemed to connect.

I know she's been going through a lot lately. Maybe she's got other stuff on her mind. Maybe she's just not interested in seeing me again. (freeze)

LIZ   We've bumped into each other a couple times. Grabbed a cup of coffee together once. That's all. We're just friends.

Last week he told me he might give me a call today just to see if I wanted to grab lunch or something. Just to talk. *(freeze)*

[Two-minute mark]

JOSH   Sometimes I get the feeling Liz is ignoring me—purposely. I just want to get together. That's all. Hang out a little bit. I really liked it when she told me about her problems—back, the first time we met.

Maybe I could help, you know? Maybe she just needs someone like me to listen to her. To care for her. *(freeze)*

LIZ   *(picks up a picture of her and her husband, sighs)* Greg and I have been married for three years . . . three years . . . *(if desired, change the number of years Liz and Greg have been married to better relate to the age of the audience.)* Sometimes it seems like a lot longer . . .

(struggling, trying to justify her actions) I just don't know if I should pick up the phone. There's nothing wrong with answering a phone call, is there? It might not even be him. *(optional: "I guess if I had caller I.D. I'd know . . .")* There's nothing wrong with just picking up the phone, right? I mean, I have to eat lunch, don't I . . . *(freeze)*

JOSH   I hope more than anything she doesn't pick up the phone. She's been toying with the idea, thinking about that other guy. Of course I know all about that. I've known about it since the beginning. *(freeze)*

[Three-minute mark]

LIZ   *(sets the picture back down, stares at the phone.)* He listened to me. He really listened. Most of the time Greg doesn't even hear what I'm saying.

From here on out, freezing while the other person speaks isn't so important since the interchanges are so quick.

JOSH   It's a choice. And picking up that phone is a step in the wrong direction.

The phone begins to ring again.

LIZ   He seemed to really care about what I'm going through. Like he understood—

JOSH   He's not the one she needs right now—

LIZ   But then there's Greg . . . and I still love him . . . at least I think I do . . . *(picks up the picture in her other hand and stares at them both, back and forth. Then, after a pause, prays)* Oh, Jesus, I don't know what to do . . .

JOSH   *(turning to look at her)* I know, Liz. I know.

Freeze. Fade out the lights as the phone continues to ring, then fade out the sound of the phone ringing until the stage is quiet.

11

TOO LATE

Why, you do not even know what will happen tomorrow. What is your life? You are a mist that appears for a little while and then vanishes.

JAMES 4:14 NIV

Brad and Kevin are paramedics whose paths cross in the hospital break room. Brad has heard about a fatality during Kevin's shift the night before. He wants to encourage him but doesn't know exactly what to say. Finally, the raw reality of death and the fleeting nature of life become apparent to both of them. And to us.

God understands when life sends us troubles and pain. He's there for us even when the answers we seek aren't. This script will help address questions such as these: Why do we pretend we're going to live forever? Why do we find it so hard to accept that our lives are brief and fleeting? How should the knowledge of our physical mortality affect our daily choices?

Time: 6 to 7 minutes

Cast

KEVIN   a twenty-seven-year-old paramedic who is struggling with the harsh realities of his job

BRAD   a thirty-four-year-old paramedic trying to encourage his younger friend

Costumes: paramedic uniforms

Props/set: chairs, cups of coffee, tables, a microwave, perhaps lockers—a typical hospital break room

Technical needs: general stage lighting, two lapel or headset microphones

Tips: Play this drama slowly. Take your time. Let each line sink in. At the beginning of the sketch, Brad is attempting some small talk to try to help Kevin, but it doesn't really work. Kevin is distracted and distant until he begins talking about the accident. Then he gets very focused and intense.

■ ■ ■

The break room at the hospital. It's 7:05 a.m. on a snowy day in November. BRAD
has been working the night shift and is getting ready to head home. KEVIN is just
coming in for the day. KEVIN is seated on stage in the break room when the lights
come up. Then BRAD enters and the sketch begins.

BRAD	*(trying to get a conversation started)* Hey, Kevin.
KEVIN	*(distracted)* Hey.
BRAD	So.
KEVIN	So.
BRAD	The Lakers *(or another professional team that might play in your area of the country during the winter)* play tonight.
KEVIN	Yeah.
BRAD	You wanna catch the game over at Greg's Sports Bar? *(or another popular local hangout)*
KEVIN	Naw. I can't. Gotta go to my daughter's play at school.
BRAD	She in school already?
KEVIN	Kindergarten.
BRAD	Kindergarten.
KEVIN	Yup. Clarice is the "Fourth Carrot on the Right" in the play.
BRAD	Fourth carrot?
KEVIN	The Fourth Carrot on the Right. That's her part.
BRAD	Huh. How many carrots are there?
KEVIN	I think about thirty.
BRAD	That's a lot of carrots.
KEVIN	Yeah and there's Broccoli too. It's a big class. Anyway, I promised her I'd go.
BRAD	You don't wanna miss those.
KEVIN	Nope.
BRAD	They grow up fast.

[One-minute mark]

KEVIN	That's what everyone says.
BRAD	*(after a pause)* Julie doing all right these days?
KEVIN	She's good. She's working again, part-time, to help pay the bills, you know.

BRAD	Yeah.
KEVIN	So we're good.
BRAD	Yeah. Good.
KEVIN	So.
BRAD	So . . . *(finally getting to the point)* Hey, Kevin, I heard about your call last night.
KEVIN	Yeah—a 316 right after the snow started. We'd just gotten back to the hospital when the call came in.
BRAD	It was a real mess out there.
KEVIN	*(intensely)* It's hard when you get there too late, Brad.
BRAD	Yeah. I know.
KEVIN	You're not too late to hear 'em, though. To hear 'em say those things they always wait too long to say. You're just too late to help 'em.

[Two-minute mark]

BRAD	I know. They always wait too long to say 'em.
KEVIN	This time it was a girl, Brad. She'd been tossed from the car. About thirty feet.
BRAD	*(intensely)* Oh boy.
KEVIN	She was still alive. There was a pool of blood all around her, you know, in the snow. Blood melting into the snow.
BRAD	Yeah. I've seen that.
KEVIN	*(detached)* The fresh blood is steamy. Then, eventually it freezes into dark red ice.
BRAD	Yeah.
KEVIN	Her blood was just starting to freeze when we got there. We couldn't do anything. She wasn't gonna make it. I mean, I could tell that right away.
BRAD	No, she wasn't, Kevin. I saw the paperwork. Don't be too hard on yourself. I—

[Three-minute mark]

KEVIN	*(interrupting BRAD)* She looked at me, Brad. She smiled at me. I could tell she was in a lot of pain. But she smiled at me anyway. She said, "It hurts, Mister," and I said, "I know," and she said, "Please help me." She wasn't even crying anymore.
BRAD	Oh, man.

KEVIN	I hate it when it's kids.
BRAD	Yeah. They're the hardest.

Long pause

BRAD	So, what did you say?
KEVIN	Huh?
BRAD	To the girl. What'd you say?
KEVIN	I told her, I says, "Yeah. I'm gonna help you. I'm not gonna let anything happen to you. It's gonna be all right." That's what I said: "I'm not gonna let anything happen to you." By then I was the one crying. I couldn't help it. And you know what?
BRAD	What?
KEVIN	She nodded at me. She just kinda smiled. She could tell, Brad.
BRAD	Tell what?

[Four-minute mark]

KEVIN	That I was lying. She could tell I was lying. Then she whispered something to me. She said, "It's OK." She told *me* it was OK. That's the last thing she said. She died a couple minutes later.
BRAD	*(opens his mouth to say something, then closes it. He can't think of anything to say)*

Long pause

KEVIN	*(distracted)* You said the Lakers are playing tonight?
BRAD	Yeah.
KEVIN	I can't watch 'em.
BRAD	I know. Your daughter's play at school.
KEVIN	How'd you know?
BRAD	You told me about it, Kevin.
KEVIN	Oh, yeah.
BRAD	She's the carrot. The fourth one on the right.
KEVIN	*(nods)* The Fourth Carrot on the Right . . . *(possible ending 1)*
	She's the same age, Clarice is. The same age as the girl in the accident last night.

[Five-minute mark]

BRAD	I hate it when you get there too late.
KEVIN	Me too.

BRAD	I know. Listen, Kevin . . . No one gets out of this alive. You can't save 'em. You can't. We're not here to do that. We're just here to help 'em the best we can. Remember the first two rules of emergency medicine they taught us back when we were training to be paramedics?
KEVIN	Rule one: everyone dies.
BRAD	Yeah. And the second one?
KEVIN	Rule two: nobody changes rule one.
BRAD	Right.
KEVIN	*(angrily)* But a little girl? Why a little girl? Why did some drunk driver have to take the life of a helpless little girl? Steal all those school plays and birthday parties and prom nights from her? Steal her whole life?

[Six-minute mark]

BRAD	I don't know.
KEVIN	It just doesn't make sense.
BRAD	I don't understand it either.
KEVIN	*(after a pause)* Brad, do you ever get used to it?
BRAD	I hope not.
KEVIN	Yeah, me too.
BRAD	*(getting up to leave)* See you tomorrow? You're ridin' with me, right?
KEVIN	Yeah. I'll see you tomorrow.
BRAD	Give your daughter a hug from me tonight, OK?
KEVIN	OK.
BRAD	Don't wait till it's too late.
KEVIN	I won't. Don't worry, Brad. I won't.

Freeze. Fade out.

12

APOLOGY ACCEPTED

And "don't sin by letting anger gain control over you." Don't let the sun go down while you are still angry.

EPHESIANS 4:26

Wendy and Alex are both practicing their apologies to each other on separate sides of the stage. Through their fumbled attempts at getting out the right words, we get a glimpse at both the argument they had and the underlying issues of forgiveness and humility.

Time: 6 minutes

Cast

WENDY   a twenty-five-year-old who's angry at her husband for calling her fat

ALEX   Wendy's twenty-seven-year-old husband who's frustrated with his nagging wife

Props/set: Two dumbbells and a jump rope (for Alex), a countertop, a kitchen knife, cabbage (for Wendy). (If Alex is in his early twenties, he could be playing a handheld video game instead of working out.)

Technical needs: two spotlights, one stage left and one stage right; two cordless lapel or headset microphones

Tips: The actors never actually address each other in this sketch but rather talk directly to the audience. Keep the exchanges quick, so the characters are each almost interrupting each other.

Both Alex and Wendy know they're partly to blame, and both know they should apologize, but neither wants to.

Wendy is in the kitchen slicing cabbage. As she gets more and more riled up, she reveals her emotion in the way she treats the vegetables—don't get too violent with the knife or it could give the wrong impression!

Alex is in the basement lifting weights. He also expresses his anger in the way he treats the weights and does his exercises.

If desired, Wendy or Alex could be trying to write a letter, transplant a house-plant, almost anything. Just don't let them get too static, stuck in one place on the stage. With whatever props you choose, the idea is to give each of them a physical way to express their inner frustrations.

■　■　■

ALEX and WENDY are both on stage as the lights come up. ALEX is standing stage left, lifting weights, WENDY is stage right, chopping veggies. Both are angry and express this physically for a few moments before any lines are spoken. They've just had an argument and have retreated into separate corners of the house to fume.

ALEX	*(angrily)* Oh!
WENDY	*(angrily)* Oh!
ALEX	I can't believe her!
WENDY	I *cannot* believe him!
ALEX	Women!
WENDY	Men!
ALEX	Oh!
WENDY	Oh!
ALEX	I mean, *she* asked me the question! She's the one who brought it up in the first place! It wasn't my fault!
WENDY	It's not like it was *my* fault or anything. All I did was ask him if he liked the red dress.
ALEX	She's like, *(twirling like a girl)* "Do you think I look fat in this dress?" What kind of question is that? So I told her.

If needed, pause to let the audience laugh.

WENDY	He said I look fat! Can you believe it!
ALEX	And then she gets mad! I mean, can you believe it?
WENDY	Even if I did look fat, he's not supposed to say so!
ALEX	What did she want me to do, lie?
WENDY	I mean, he could have lied at least a little bit. *(angry again)* Oh!

[One-minute mark]

ALEX	So then, that's just the beginning, right? *(deliver this next section quickly, in one breath)* So then I just *mention* how she's overreacting and how she has no right to get mad at me since she's the one who's always getting on my case by nagging me all the time. I just mention it, and she goes totally crazy!
WENDY	No matter how much I try to help him by just pointing out what work he needs to do around the house, he goes crazy!

This next section is a rapid-fire interchange as their words almost overlap each other.

ALEX	I mean, it's nag, nag, nag, nag, nag—
WENDY	Like that bookcase he never finished building in the basement—
ALEX	Nag! Nag! Nag!—
WENDY	And the tree house *(or playhouse)* he keeps telling the kids he's gonna build—
ALEX	Nag! Nag! Nag!—
WENDY	Not to mention the lawn hasn't been mowed in three weeks!
ALEX	Nag! Nag! Nag! Nag!—
WENDY	It's not like I'm nagging him. I'm just trying to be helpful.
ALEX	It'd be helpful if she just left me alone once in a while!
WENDY	I oughtta just leave him alone once in a while. That'd teach him!

Both pace angrily in unison, unaware that their spouse is pacing in another part of the house.

ALEX	She's always accusing me of everything!

[Two-minute mark]

WENDY	He's always accusing me of everything.
ALEX	Oh!
WENDY	Oh!

Both pace some more.

ALEX	And she's such a neat freak!
WENDY	He's such a slob! At least I like being organized!
ALEX	She alphabetizes the spices! *(after a pause)* Oh, and she gets so defensive all the time!
WENDY	He just attacks me! All he ever does is complain!
ALEX	All she ever does is nag! And she *totally* refuses to apologize!

WENDY	He never admits he was wrong about anything! He just doesn't understand women.
ALEX	I just don't understand women. *(after a pause)* I wish *just once in a while* she could see things from my point of view! Next, she'll probably bring up the past.
WENDY	He does this all the time! Just last week he argued with me about the stupid toilet seat.

[Three-minute mark]

ALEX	Like with the toilet seat. I mean, why does it have to be my job to put it down! Why can't it be her job to leave it up!
WENDY	That, and he's always stealing the covers!
ALEX	She's always forgetting to recharge the cell phone!
WENDY	Oh!
ALEX	Oh!

After a pause, calming down somewhat

WENDY	*(fingering her ring)* The thing is, though, I still love him.
ALEX	*(sigh)* But . . . I really do love her.
WENDY	*(sigh)*
ALEX	Man, I hate it when we argue like this.
WENDY	I can't stand when this stuff happens.
ALEX	I wonder if these arguments bug her like they do me.
WENDY	I wonder if it bothers him as much as it does me.
ALEX	Because I really love her.
WENDY	Because I really love him.
ALEX	OK, maybe I should apologize.
WENDY	I guess I could say I'm sorry. OK, let's see . . .

[Four-minute mark]

ALEX	All right, all right. Let's see . . . *(practicing to an imaginary WENDY)* "Wendy. I'm sorry . . . that you're so sensitive about your weight . . ."
WENDY	He always makes his apologies seem like our problems are all my fault.
ALEX	No, that's no good. It almost makes it sound like it was all her fault.

WENDY   Let's see . . . what should I say . . ."Alex, I'm sorry that you don't listen the first time when I ask you to do something and that I have to repeat it a hundred times before you even get your big, fat, lazy butt up off the couch."

ALEX   She'll probably accuse me of being lazy.

WENDY   No, that's not it.

In this exchange, emphasize the word "if."

ALEX   How about, "I'm sorry if I hurt your feelings."

WENDY   I hate it when he says, "I'm sorry *if*, blah, blah, blah . . ." What kind of an apology is that? *If!*

ALEX   No, that's not quite it.

In this exchange, emphasize the word "but."

[Five-minute mark]

WENDY   How 'bout, "Alex, I'm sorry, but I've just been under a lot of stress lately."

ALEX   I can't stand it when she says, "I'm sorry, *but.*" That's not an apology! It's just a way to set up for an excuse!

WENDY   I'm sorry.

ALEX   I'm sorry.

WENDY   Sorry.

ALEX   Sorry.

TOGETHER   I'm sorry.

WENDY   Just those two words. Maybe that's all I need to say.

ALEX   I wonder what she'd say to that, if I just said I was sorry.

WENDY   I wonder what he'd do if I just told him "I'm sorry." No rationalizing. No excuses. Nothing.

ALEX   Not trying to justify myself. Just saying I'm sorry. Just that simple. She'd probably freak out.

WENDY   He'd probably go into shock.

ALEX   Why is it so hard to say those two words?

[Possible ending 1]

WENDY   *(sensitively, to God)* Oh, God, please, God. I want to say it. I do. It's just so hard.

ALEX   *(to God)* God, I don't know how to do this.

[Six-minute mark]

WENDY	It's really tough—
ALEX	To admit—
WENDY	To say those words—
ALEX	I was wrong—
WENDY	I'm sorry.
ALEX	But that's what I need to say . . .
WENDY	That's what I need to do . . .

ALEX sets down the weights, WENDY sets down the knifes and vegetables.

IN UNISON	OK, here goes nothing . . .

Turn toward each other and freeze as the lights fade out.

PART FOUR

PORTRAITS

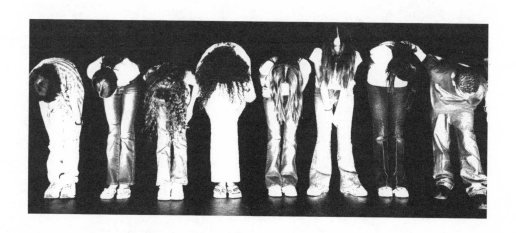

13

THE KINGDOM

You have been permitted to understand the secrets of the Kingdom of God. But I am using these stories to conceal everything about it from outsiders.

LUKE 8:10

During this series of brief vignettes interwoven with Scripture readings, the audience will get a fresh look at some of Jesus' parables. They'll also be able to reflect on what it really means to pursue the kingdom of God.

Time: Each vignette is 2 to 3 minutes long.

Cast

Two actors and two actresses, **PHIL** and **BRENDAN**, **WHITNEY** and **ESTHER**, share a series of brief vignettes and Scripture readings based on some of the parables of Jesus.

Technical needs: general stage lighting and four cordless lapel or headset microphones

Tips: Begin with Brendan and Phil positioned on center stage, Whitney just left of center stage, and Esther just right of center. For the first scene they will serve as the announcers. For each scene, the announcers freeze while the scene plays out on center stage.

The setting varies for each vignette. If desired, project the titles of each scene on the screen up front as the narrator announces it. Be aware of managing your props so they don't become unwieldy. If desired, move to different places on stage and have the different scenes already set up there. The Bible readings included at the end of each vignette are optional and could be done as a voice-over or even projected on the screen.

You could use music stands for the two announcers, standing just right and left of center. Then, the announcers could just read their parables from black folders.

■　■　■

Optional introduction to the vignettes (based on Luke 13:17-18)

BRENDAN	The people were delighted with Jesus and all the wonderful things he was doing.
ESTHER	One day he turned to the crowd and said:
PHIL	"What is the kingdom of God like? What shall I compare it to?"
WHITNEY	Maybe if he were talking to us today, he would tell his story like this . . .

■ ■ ■

Scene 1: The Parable of the Cheap Boyfriend

Props/set: A glass display counter from a jewelry store (optional)

In this scene BRENDAN plays a young man looking for a good deal on a ring for his girlfriend (or wife, depending on the age of your audience). PHIL plays a condescending salesperson at an upscale jewelry store.

ESTHER	*(to the audience)* The parable of the cheap boyfriend. *(freeze)*
BRENDAN	*(entering)* Hello, I'm, um . . . I'm looking for just the right present for a very special girl *(or "woman")*.
PHIL	Of course. And do you have a price in mind?
BRENDAN	Um. Twenty bucks or so. Wal-Mart had a lot of good stuff in that price range. I'm comparison shopping.
PHIL	Of course. Sir, I believe you may be in the wrong store.
BRENDAN	What do you mean?
PHIL	The jewelry we carry is of a much—how shall I say—higher quality.
BRENDAN	So you think I'm cheap.
PHIL	In a word, yes.
BRENDAN	Well, then Mr. Higher-Quality-in-a-Word-Yes, how much should I expect to pay for a killer ring for my girlfriend?
PHIL	Well, that depends. *(feel free to increase the amounts if dictated by your local economy)* Eight or ten thousand would get you an acceptable piece of jewelry. And we can go up from there.

[One-minute mark]

BRENDAN	You mean to tell me that you sell jewelry for as much as I make at work in six months! *(once again, change the length of time he'd have to work, if necessary)*
PHIL	Well, the question for you, sir, is simple.
BRENDAN	Oh, yeah? What's that?
PHIL	Is she worth it? I mean, how much is she worth to you?
BRENDAN	Hmm . . . I get your drift. The right answer isn't twenty bucks is it?
PHIL	I should hope not, sir. I should hope not.
Freeze	
WHITNEY	"The Kingdom of Heaven is like a pearl merchant on the lookout for choice pearls.
ESTHER	"When he discovered a pearl of great value, he sold everything he owned and bought it!" *(Matthew 13:45-46)*
WHITNEY AND ESTHER	*(in unison)* "Anyone who is willing to hear should listen and understand!" *(Luke 8:8)*

■ ■ ■

Scene 2: The Parable of the Sales Fliers

Props/set: Two or three bags filled with clothes from Victoria's Secret or another lingerie store

In this scene BRENDAN plays a guy annoyed at his wife's shopping habits. ESTHER plays his frugal wife who is always on the lookout for a good deal. Before beginning, PHIL and ESTHER switch places so that BRENDAN and ESTHER are center stage.

PHIL	*(to the audience)* The parable of the sales fliers. *(freeze)*
ESTHER	*(setting down two or three bags from the mall)*
BRENDAN	*(entering)* Hey, Esther. How was your trip to the mall?
ESTHER	*(excited)* Great! There was a sale at Victoria's Secret! *(or another local lingerie store)* I just saved over $41!
BRENDAN	Man, I don't know how you always find out about these sales you're . . . Did you say Victoria's Secret?
ESTHER	*(turns the bag so he can see the label)* Uh-huh.

BRENDAN	*(eyes getting really big)* You went shopping there?
ESTHER	*(nod)* Mm-hm.
BRENDAN	They had a sale?
ESTHER	Yup.
BRENDAN	And the stuff you bought is in that bag right there?
ESTHER	That's right. I got a lot of good stuff. See? *(opens up the bag and lets him peer inside)*
BRENDAN	Oh boy, oh boy, oh boy . . .
ESTHER	It was all on sale, but if you need me to, I can take this stuff back . . .
BRENDAN	*(still looking in the bag)* I think we can manage . . .
ESTHER	*(taking the bags from him)* Oh good. I was hoping you'd say that because the sale was today only.
BRENDAN	How do you always find out about these one-day sales things? It's like you have some kind of internal sales-event radar or something.
ESTHER	I get little fliers in the mail. Reminders. Stuff like that.
BRENDAN	I always throw that stuff out.
ESTHER	Most people do. *(clutching the bag)* But if you read 'em and actually show up at the store, you get to reap the benefits . . .
BRENDAN	Yeah, and so do I . . .

Freeze.

WHITNEY	"A farmer went out to plant some seed. As he scattered it across his field, some seed fell on a footpath . . .
PHIL	"Other seed fell on shallow soil with underlying rock . . .
WHITNEY	"Other seed fell among thorns . . .
PHIL	"Still other seed fell on fertile soil. This seed grew and produced a crop one hundred times as much as had been planted." *(Luke 8:5-8)*
WHITNEY AND PHIL	*(in unison)* "Anyone who is willing to hear should listen and understand!" *(Luke 8:8)*

■ ■ ■

Scene 3: The Parable of the Diaper Rash

Props/set: A tube of diaper-rash ointment and a tube of toothpaste (try to get tubes that look similar), a toothbrush

In this scene PHIL plays a guy who nearly brushed his teeth with the baby's diaper rash ointment. WHITNEY plays his insightful wife.

PHIL and WHITNEY switch places with BRENDAN and ESTHER.

BRENDAN	*(to the audience)* The parable of the diaper rash. *(freeze)*
PHIL	*(entering, carrying the toothbrush and two tubes)* Whitney, you know what?
WHITNEY	What's that, Phil?
PHIL	Diaper-rash cream should not be packaged in a tube that looks like toothpaste.
WHITNEY	What are you talking about?
PHIL	I'll never have diaper rash on my tongue again.
WHITNEY	You didn't really!
PHIL	No, but I did squeeze it onto my brush. I stopped just short of oral application.
WHITNEY	*(comparing the tubes)* I had no idea they looked so much alike!
PHIL	Yeah, well I guess some things aren't exactly what they appear to be. Makes me wonder how many times I've smeared Colgate *(or the brand you're using)* on the baby's bottom.
WHITNEY	I don't even wanna think about it.
PHIL	Me neither. Maybe we oughtta just throw out the diaper-rash stuff. I mean, so we don't mix 'em up again.
WHITNEY	When she's out of diapers we can. Until then, you'll just need to read the label better, OK?
PHIL	I guess.
WHITNEY	'Cause I'm not kissing you if you get 'em mixed up.
PHIL	Huh, I wouldn't kiss me either . . .

Freeze.

BRENDAN	"The Kingdom of Heaven is like a farmer who planted good seed in his field. But that night as everyone slept, his enemy came and planted weeds among the wheat.

ESTHER	"When the crop began to grow and produce grain, the weeds also grew. The farmer's servants came and told him, 'Sir, the field where you planted that good seed is full of weeds!'
BRENDAN	" 'An enemy has done it!' the farmer exclaimed.
ESTHER	" 'Shall we pull out the weeds?' they asked.
BRENDAN	"He replied, 'No, you'll hurt the wheat if you do. Let both grow together until the harvest. Then I will tell the harvesters to sort out the weeds and burn them and to put the wheat in the barn.' " *(Matthew 13:24-30)*
ESTHER AND BRENDAN	*(in unison)* "Anyone who is willing to hear should listen and understand!" *(Luke 8:8)*

■ ■ ■

Scene 4: The Parable of the Canned Employee

Props/set: A water cooler and small paper cups

In this scene BRENDAN is sharing office gossip around the water cooler with PHIL, who hasn't heard the latest news.

PHIL and ESTHER switch places.

WHITNEY	*(to the audience)* The parable of the canned employee. *(freeze)*
BRENDAN	So did you hear about Anderson?
PHIL	No, what happened?
BRENDAN	Got canned.
PHIL	What? Why?
BRENDAN	Well, Richards just got back from that business trip, right?
PHIL	Yeah, to the convention in L.A.—
BRENDAN	Right. Well, he got back a day early and decided to swing by the office. He caught Anderson red-handed downloading company files.
PHIL	You're kiddin'!
BRENDAN	Nope. He's been doin' it all the time, I guess. He also had copyrighted movies and mp3 files on there. With the whole integrity thing in businesses today, they came down on him pretty hard.
PHIL	Wow.

BRENDAN	And the kicker is, you know what Anderson's job was, don't you?
PHIL	Yeah. CFO.
BRENDAN	Yup, Chief Financial Officer. Richards had left all the company finances in the hands of a thief.
PHIL	When the cat's away, the mice will play.
BRENDAN	I guess so.

Both guys drink their water as the lights fade out.

ESTHER	"You must be ready all the time, for the Son of Man will come when least expected . . .
WHITNEY	"If the master returns and finds that the servant has done a good job, there will be a reward . . .
ESTHER	"But if the servant thinks, 'My master won't be back for a while,' and begins oppressing the other servants, partying, and getting drunk—well, the master will return unannounced and unexpected.
WHITNEY	"He will tear the servant apart and banish him with the unfaithful. The servant will be severely punished, for though he knew his duty, he refused to do it." *(Luke 12:40, 43, 45-47)*
WHITNEY AND ESTHER	*(in unison)* "Anyone who is willing to hear should listen and understand!" *(Luke 8:8)*

▪ ▪ ▪

Scene 5: The Parable of the Pink Underwear

Props/set: A clothes basket full of clean laundry (both whites and colors)

In this scene WHITNEY is presenting a monologue. She should be on center stage, BRENDAN and ESTHER step to one side, and PHIL steps to the other.

PHIL	*(to the audience)* The parable of the pink underwear *(or "boxer shorts," freeze)*
WHITNEY	*(upset)* Huh. "Be sure to sort the laundry," I said. "Be sure to wash the whites with the whites and the colors with the colors." That's not so tough, is it? Those aren't terribly confusing instructions, are they? And does he do it? No. He mixes 'em all together and tosses one giant load into the washer. I'm gonna have to make laundry off limits to him. This is the third time.

(holding up pink boxer shorts, smirking) I'm going to pack these in his workout bag. He'll make quite an impression on the guys at the gym.

(sighing) Yeah, the two colors can sit next to each other in the drawer, or hang next to each other in the closet. That's all good and fine. But there comes a time when you gotta separate 'em. They just don't mix together well in the end. *(freeze)*

BRENDAN   "The Kingdom of Heaven is like a fishing net that is thrown into the water and gathers fish of every kind.

ESTHER   "When the net is full, they drag it up onto the shore, sit down, sort the good fish into crates, and throw the bad ones away.

PHIL   "That is the way it will be at the end of the world. The angels will come and separate the wicked people from the godly, throwing the wicked into the fire. There will be weeping and gnashing of teeth." *(Mathew 13:47-50)*

WHITNEY   "Anyone who is willing to hear should listen and understand!" *(Luke 8:8)*

Freeze. Fade out.

14

BIGGER BARNS

Yes, a person is a fool to store up earthly wealth but not have a rich relationship with God.

LUKE 12:21

In this contemporary adaptation of Jesus' parable of the foolish rich man, we see how easy it is to get lured away from Christ by the comforts, riches and pleasures of this life. With possibilities for a multimedia presentation, this thought-provoking drama brings home the impact of Jesus' story to contemporary listeners.

Time: 7 to 8 minutes

Cast

NARRATOR   (could be a prerecorded voiceover)

RICH MAN   (mid-fifties), a contemporary example of the foolish rich man in Jesus' parable—rich and powerful, but not committed to godly priorities

GABE   (mid-twenties), a successful young businessman who has big plans

LISA   (mid-twenties), Gabe's supportive and optimistic wife

KATIE   (four to six years old; could be a prerecorded voiceover), Gabe and Lisa's oldest daughter

Props/set: two chairs, glasses (or another simple costume piece), wine glasses and table setting from a fancy restaurant, musician's stool (if you use a live narrator)

Technical needs: four spotlights, three cordless lapel or headset microphones and one handheld microphone. Katie uses the handheld mic offstage (or you could prerecord her part and play it as a voiceover). Direct one spot on stage left, one on center stage, one just right of center (on the table setting) and one on the musician's stool on stage right. (This spot isn't used until the end of the drama, and then only if you use an onstage narrator.)

This sketch has an optional video at the end. If you have the capability, it would make a very powerful addition to the drama. If you choose to include the video at the end of the presentation, you'll need to film your actors at the appropriate locations prior to performing this sketch.

You'll also need a prerecorded sound of tires screeching and a car crashing.

Tips: Everything seems to be going right for Gabe and Lisa. The tension develops as the audience realizes something bad is going to happen. The rug is about to be pulled out from under them. They have big plans, but God never appears on the radar screen of their lives.

Make sure that the Rich Man and the couple come across sympathetically to the listeners. They should be genuine, sincere people with whom your audience can identify. They're not stuck-up or overly materialistic. You want them to be people just like us.

Work on the timing of the lights and sound for the collision scene at the end of the drama. The last thing you want is for that scene to seem cheesy or poorly choreographed.

Use a slight costume change, such as slipping glasses on or off, or changing accessories to help designate the progression of time from one scene to the next for Gabe and Lisa.

■ ■ ■

LISA and GABE act out four different scenes. Each is described in the notes within the script. The narrator shouldn't be on stage yet.

The RICH MAN is located on stage left, LISA and GABE are on center stage. Just right of center, in the shadows, is a table set for a fancy restaurant. On the right side of the stage is a musician's stool (out of sight).

The RICH MAN freezes while the couple performs their lines. They freeze while he says his. All three are on stage, frozen, when the lights come up and the sketch begins.

Dim the spotlight on center stage, bring up the one on stage left.

RICH MAN   I guess all I ever really wanted was to be comfortable. You know? That's all, just comfortable. That's why I worked so hard. Put in the extra hours. Sacrificed. That's why I tried so hard to manage my money wisely. I just wanted to experience the good things in life. *(freeze)*

Dim the spotlight on stage left, bring up the one on center stage.

■ ■ ■

Scene 1

6:22 p.m. Monday evening. LISA is at the apartment when GABE comes through the door. They are in their early twenties and newly married. He's just been to a job interview and she wants to know how it went.

LISA   So honey, how'd it go?

GABE   *(feigning sadness)* Well . . . I've got some good news and some bad news.

LISA   Oh, no. What's the good news?

GABE   Well, the good news is that I made it to the interview on time, even though there was a wreck on I-81. *(or another local highway)*

LISA   *(hesitantly)* And the bad news?

GABE   *(suddenly excited)* They couldn't find anyone else for the job, so they decided to offer it to me!

LISA   *(swatting him)* Oh, you! *(excited)* So, you *got* it! You got the job!

GABE   Yeah! Mr. Freeman said he wants me to start the first of the month!

LISA   Well, that's great!

GABE   Yeah.

LISA   So all your hard work finally paid off?

GABE   I guess so!

[One-minute mark]

LISA   I can't believe it! I'm *so* excited!

GABE   Yeah, me too. Things are gonna to be a lot easier for us from now on.

LISA and GABE freeze. Dim the spotlight on center stage, bring up the one on stage left.

RICH MAN   I didn't live a lavish lifestyle, nothing like that. I was just trying to make a living. You know. Be smart. Invest wisely. *(walks and looks around.)* Started working here in the summers back in high school, worked my way up over the years. Sales. Then district manager, V.P., and finally, CEO. *(freeze)*

Dim the spotlight on stage left; bring up the one on center stage.

■   ■   ■

Scene 2

Ten months later. LISA and GABE are looking around a new house in the suburbs; they want to buy it and move up in the world, but they're not sure they can afford it.

LISA	*(looking around at the house)* Oh, this place is incredible!
GABE	Yeah. No kidding.
LISA	And look, look, look! You can see the mountains *(or ocean)* from here!
GABE	Whoa.
LISA	*(after a pause)* So . . . can we really afford it?
GABE	Well, it's not gonna be easy, Lisa. I may have to do a little more traveling.
LISA	Yeah.

[Two-minute mark]

GABE	For the last six months or so, Freeman's been asking me to help set up a new account in Atlanta *(or another city in a nearby state)*.
LISA	Yeah, I know.
GABE	Just to make ends meet and everything. It doesn't have to be forever.
LISA	No, of course not.
GABE	So, yeah, I think we can do it.
LISA	*(hesitantly)* It'll be a longer commute if we move out here.
GABE	I know, but it's closer to the airport. And look at the view! And the yard!
LISA	Yeah, our kids are gonna love it.
GABE	Kids? Our kids?
LISA	*(sweetly)* Well, someday.
GABE	Yeah, someday. You were scaring me there for a minute.
LISA	*(flirty)* But Gabe, I thought you weren't scared of anything? Is my big strong man scared of a little baby?
GABE	Babies, no. Diapers, yes.

LISA and GABE freeze. Dim the spotlight on center stage; bring up the one on stage left.

RICH MAN	So one day I got the news. Good news. My accountants couldn't believe it! I mean the way the markets had been going the last couple years no one expected such a quick turnaround. But our position in the marketplace was unprecedented. I guess you could say we were in the right place at the right time.

[Three-minute mark]

Dim the spotlight on stage left, bring up the one positioned on the table setting just right of center stage.

■ ■ ■

Scene 3

Six years later. LISA and GABE have gone out for supper. They now have two children. Fade out the spot on center; bring up the spot on the table.

GABE	Oh, man. I am so glad your parents came to town this weekend.
LISA	You're glad my parents are visiting?
GABE	Oh yeah.
LISA	Hmm, I never thought I'd hear you say that.
GABE	Well, they're watching the kids for us tonight, aren't they?
LISA	Yeah. *(sweetly)* So we can go on a date. Just the two of us. No kids.
GABE	Let's not talk about the kids, OK.
LISA	OK.
GABE	So, what do you want to talk about?
LISA	I don't know. What about you?
GABE	I don't know.
LISA	I wonder if the kids are OK.
GABE	They're fine, Lisa.
LISA	*(pulling out her cell phone)* Maybe I should call. Just to check in.
GABE	*(pushing her cell phone to the side)* Hey, let's just enjoy this night, OK? Just the two of us.
LISA	OK. *(after a pause)* So—
GABE	So, Lisa . . . *(smiling)* we're doing it.
LISA	I know. I can hardly believe it.
GABE	We've got a nice house, awesome kids, jobs we love.

| LISA | (*sweetly, taking his hand*) We've got each other. |
| GABE | Yeah. |

[Four-minute mark]

| LISA | We're living our dream, aren't we? |
| GABE | The Great American Dream, yeah. I guess you could say (*slowly, distinctly*) everything is going according to plan. |

LISA and GABE freeze. Dim the spotlight aimed just right of center stage, bring up the one on stage left.

| RICH MAN | Anyway, our warehouses weren't even big enough to handle the demand. Our whole corporate infrastructure would need to expand. Open another office in Singapore. Maybe one in Frankfurt. With the right kind of planning, we could capture 17 to 18 percent of the market share by this time next year. I'd be able to retire early. Take it easy. Relax. Enjoy myself. Yeah, (*slowly, distinctly*) everything was going according to plan. (*turns his back to the audience and freezes, or, if staging dictates it, exits*) |

Fade out the spotlight on stage left; bring up the one positioned on the table setting just right of center stage.

■ ■ ■

Scene 4

An hour later. LISA and GABE are driving home from supper—don't do any costume change. As the lights are changing, turn the chairs to face the audience. GABE is driving, sitting stage left of LISA.

LISA	Hey, that place was really good.
GABE	Yeah. We'll have to go back, try the chicken Kiev next time.
LISA	Yeah.
GABE	(*check your watch.*) So it's not too late yet. You wanna catch a movie?
LISA	I was hoping you'd ask.
GABE	There's this great suspense thriller that just came out.

[Five-minute mark]

LISA	I was thinking of a romance.
GABE	A romance? I'm not really a big fan of—
LISA	C'mon, Gabe, you know romance movies always get me in the mood . . .

GABE	A romance movie sounds good.
LISA	Thought so. *(pulling out cell phone)* I'm gonna call, just to check in on the kids. Let Mom know we're gonna be a little late.
GABE	OK.
LISA	*(to cell phone)* Hey. Yeah, this is Lisa. How are the kids, Mom? *(pause; aside, to GABE)* Everything's fine.
GABE	I told you not to worry.
LISA	*(to cell phone)* Yeah, supper was good. We're gonna catch a movie and then come home. OK. Oh, *(aside, to GABE)* the kids wanna say goodnight.
GABE	It figures.
LISA	*(to cell phone)* Hi, Katie. Mommy loves you. Hugs and kisses. Goodnight, sweetie. Can you give the phone to your sist— *(aside, to GABE)* she wants to say goodnight to her daddy . . . Here . . . *(hands the phone to GABE)*
GABE	Hey, Katie . . .

GABE tucks the phone under his chin. While he's talking with KATIE, LISA flips down the sun visor and touches up her makeup in the little mirror.

| GABE | *(still driving, distracted, talking on the phone)* . . . No, honey, I can't tell you a bedtime story 'cause I'm driving down the road . . . I *(sighing)* OK, look, look, look . . . um, once upon a time there was a princess named Katie . . . Yeah, I know that's your name . . . and one day she fought against this giant dragon, um, who was burning up the villages— |

[Six-minute mark]

LISA	It's a bedtime story, Gabe!
GABE	Oh, yeah. Right. Um, burning up the villages—but all the people were safe at the mall 'cause there was a concert there or something . . . *(slower)* and then, all of a sudden—
LISA	*(flip the visor back up just in time to see the oncoming semi swerve into your lane.)* Gabe! A truck! Look out for that truck!
GABE	Ahh! *(spin the steering wheel. Freeze. Possible ending 1)*

Both GABE and LISA throw their arms up to protect their faces and freeze. Blackout to the sound of screeching tires and a sickening crash. As the sound of the crash fades, KATIE's voice comes across the sound system. She's still talking on the cell phone: "Daddy? Daddy? Are you there, Daddy? Are you OK? Daddy, what happened? How does the story end, Daddy? Daddy?"

[Seven-minute mark]

NARRATOR enters during the blackout and sits on stage right, LISA and GABE exit in the dark. Lights come up on the NARRATOR. Or you could just use a voiceover for this part and bring up a video of GABE and LISA at their first apartment, at their new home in the suburbs, at a fancy local restaurant, then walking toward their car and, at the end of the voiceover, show images of a funeral or two gravestones.

NARRATOR *(reading from the Bible)* Then someone called from the crowd, "Teacher, please tell my brother to divide our father's estate with me."

Jesus replied, "Friend, who made me a judge over you to decide such things as that?" Then he said, "Beware! Don't be greedy for what you don't have. Real life is not measured by how much we own."

And he gave an illustration: "A rich man had a fertile farm that produced fine crops. In fact, his barns were full to overflowing. So he said, 'I know! I'll tear down my barns and build bigger ones. Then I'll have room enough to store everything. And I'll sit back and say to myself, My friend, you have enough stored away for years to come. Now take it easy! Eat, drink, and be merry!'

"But God said to him, 'You fool! You will die this very night. Then who will get it all?'

"Yes, a person is a fool to store up earthly wealth but not have a rich relationship with God." (Luke 12:13-21)

Close the Bible. Freeze. Fade out.

15

THE FIRE WITHIN

But if I say, "I will not mention him

or speak any more in his name,"

his word is in my heart like a fire,

a fire shut up in my bones.

I am weary of holding it in;

indeed, I cannot.

JEREMIAH 20:9 NIV

Three narrators explore how religion and worship fit together in this image-rich, interpretive reading. By the end both the narrators and the listeners will have a clearer picture of what lies at the heart of truly worshiping God. This reflective and worshipful piece will serve well to introduce the question of what worship really is.

Time: 3 to 4 minutes

Cast

Three storytellers, **BARB**, **RAMON** and **ALI**, weave their insights together in this reflective, interpretive piece. The names of the narrators aren't significant to the flow of this piece. Your narrators could be either female or male, though it might be wise to have a mixture of male and females to more naturally appeal to a broader audience.

Costumes: casual, contemporary, neutral clothes (such as a black turtleneck and jeans)

Props/set: candles, matches, a candlelight dinner table setting (or hang-out chair and table at a coffee shop), a streetlamp (or a lamp and a light bulb), a step ladder, a church pew

Technical needs: general stage lighting or selected spots on the three storytellers, and three cordless lapel or headset microphones

Tips: The actors are not addressing each other in this sketch but are talking directly to the audience. Because of that, they won't ever make eye contact with each other but will look at the audience instead.

All three of the narrators for this piece are in a place where candles (or light) play a significant role.

Consider having a musician play quiet, airy instrumental music in the background during this drama.

■ ■ ■

When blocking this sketch, explore levels and light. For example, RAMONA (stage left) could be setting a candlelight dinner for two, ALI (center stage) could be halfway up a stepladder fixing a streetlamp (or replacing a light blub on the ceiling of the stage), and BARB (right stage) could be at a coffee shop next to a lamp, or kneeling beside a church pew surrounded by candles. All are caught, as it were, in a moment of their lives.

All three narrators are on stage in their different settings when the lights come up and the drama begins.

This first confessional section is optional and could be dropped if you wish to move right into the poetic reflections on worship.

RAMONA	Once, long ago, I set my religion on a shelf—
BARB	Where I could keep a good eye on it—
ALI	And it wouldn't be able to stick its nose in where it didn't belong.
BARB	And over the years I pretty much forgot it was even there.
RAMONA	Oh, I pulled it out once or twice—
ALI	To show it to people I was trying to impress.
BARB	But it wasn't really very impressive at all.
RAMONA	Now dust has gathered thick and still.
ALI	And time has totally dried it out.
BARB	It doesn't really look like my religion anymore.
RAMONA	It doesn't look like much of *anything* anymore—
ALI	Just kinda looks like the withered remains of a lifeless human heart.

[One-minute mark]

After a brief pause

RAMONA   Oh, I've tasted all the streams that flow from the sacred books.

BARB	The mythic and the magic.
ALI	The ancient and the new.
RAMONA	But none of them have been able to quench my thirst.
BARB	They just leave me more disillusioned and thirstier than ever—
ALI	For what's real.

After a brief pause

BARB	What I need isn't another religion—
ALI	A set of more rules, a book of old laws—
RAMONA	A system—
BARB	Or a philosophy—
ALI	Or a new worldview.
RAMONA	I've tried them all on for size, but none of them seem to fit.
BARB	They're all too loose around the waist or too tight up here in the shoulders.
ALI	No, I need something else.
BARB	Fresh.
RAMONA	Living.
ALI	Relational.
BARB	Real.
RAMONA	A story that's strong enough to conquer the past.
ALI	A truth that's woven with wonder and love.

After a brief pause

RAMONA	I beat my wings against the bars of my cage.
ALI	I don't even know where the key is anymore.
BARB	Maybe I never even had one.

Say the following section differently, as a poem. If desired, have your actors cross the stage as they say these lines.

RAMONA	O, is there a flame that can scatter the night?
BARB	A prayer in my soul that awakens the light?
ALI	O, is there a fire that rises unseen?
RAMONA	Or water that's able to quench and to clean?

[Two-minute mark]

After a brief pause

ALI	There are moments, only moments, when I think I'm finally beginning to understand.
BARB	When the veil is lifted and the mystery begins to unfold.
RAMONA	When God and worship finally make sense to me.
ALI	When I begin to realize what it all really means.
BARB	It's not about rules and rituals—
RAMONA	Candles and sacrifices—
ALI	Churches and sermons—
BARB	Or slick TV evangelists with big hair.
RAMONA	That's all smoke from an extinguished fire.
BARB	*(picks up a candle)* I think worship is more like the taste of desire on lover's lips—
ALI	The call of a loon over northern lakes—
RAMONA	The cry of a child at her mother's breast—
BARB	The fragrance of mountains on the edge of the wind.
ALI	Alive.
BARB	Free.
ALI	Nourishing.
RAMONA	Intoxicating.
BARB	Now, that comes closer to the heart of the matter—
ALI	Closer to the real essence of worship.

[Three-minute mark]

RAMONA	It's a fire that consumes your soul—
ALI	A blossom of life that finally breaks through the crusty snows—
BARB	Of religion.

Treat this last portion as a prayer.

RAMONA	O Spirit unseen.
ALI	O Creator unrivaled.
BARB	O Savior of seekers and Finder of the lost—
RAMONA	I search and I search and I search—
ALI	And at last I find you.
BARB	Finding me.
ALI	At last I discover you.

RAMONA	Discovering me—
BARB	Here, in this moment—
RAMONA	Where love touches life.
BARB	And worship becomes real—
ALI	Fire beyond fire.
RAMONA	Light-giving light.
BARB	Pathway to freedom and truth.
RAMONA	Few walk there.
ALI	The flame is too hot.
BARB	Let me walk that road—
ALI	And discover what it means—
RAMONA	To truly believe—
BARB	And to enter the final mystery—
ALI	Of faith.

Freeze. Fade out. Transition to worship music or to the message.

16

Ripples in the Divine Sea

God has made everything beautiful for its own time. He has
planted eternity in the human heart, but even so, people cannot
see the whole scope of God's work from beginning to end.

ECCLESIASTES 3:11

In this unique presentation, two narrators share a series of poetic reflections on worship and the human experience. This script would work well as a voiceover (either live, or prerecorded with music) and presented during a video presentation.

Use this script to prepare for worship or to explore questions such as: How can we humans, as flawed as we are, ever bring glory to God? Does he really accept us as is? Do we even matter to God—and if so, how would our lives be different if we really lived like it?

Time: 3 to 4 minutes

Cast

Two storytellers, **MATTHEW** and **CHERISE** (they could be two males or two females), weave their insights together in this reflective, interpretive piece. If desired, you could have up to six narrators present this piece.

Costumes: casual, contemporary, neutral clothes (such as a black turtleneck and jeans)

Props/set: video and music to complement the poetic readings

Technical needs: general stage lighting or spots on the two storytellers, and two cordless lapel or headset microphones. (This drama could include six narrators. If so, you'll need six microphones.) The entire drama could be done as a voiceover with inspiring images projected on the screen up front.

Tips: This drama is really a collection of poetic readings meant to be woven in with worship music, dance, mime or video. Some churches may not have the capability to present such a program. If not, you may wish to present it simply as a reader's theater piece with background music. Give your readers black folders that contain the script and have them read their parts while either seated on musician's stools or standing on stage.

The actors are not addressing each other in this sketch but are talking directly to the audience. If you choose to use six readers instead of two, position them in different places on stage and simply assign a different poem (or section of a poem) to each of them.

Consider having a musician play quiet, reflective instrumental music in the background during this presentation.

■ ■ ■

If you are using live readers, the narrators are on stage when the lights come up and the presentation begins. Otherwise, if you're using voiceovers, no one will be on stage.

Video idea: project images of a newborn with a parent or grandparent, and then at the end of the poem, project the word "life" onto the screen, then fade away or transition to the next reading and set of images.

MATTHEW   the maze of this moment
is speckled with blood and spotted with tears
i hear them chime together, in unison,
to create this melody we call life.

Video idea: project images of a person walking in a field or along a beach, and then at the end of the poem, project the word "comfort" onto the screen; then fade away or transition to the next reading and set of images.

CHERISE   i want to be noticed,
yet so often i feel alone.
overlooked.
unloved.
yet there is no greater love than yours
which reaches down with a father's hand
to wipe every tear from my eye.
unnoticed.

Video idea: project images of galaxies and the stars, and then at the end of the poem, project the word "regrets" onto the screen; then fade away or transition to the next reading and set of images.

MATTHEW   in the beginning
your breath brought life to the empty darkness
and gave light to a lonely universe
i wonder what you will do to the dark expanse of my past,
when you whisper your presence into my soul.

[One-minute mark]

Video idea: project images of a dandelion blowing in the wind or sand flowing in the desert, and then at the end of the poem, project the word "forgiveness" onto the screen; then fade away or transition to the next reading and set of images.

CHERISE   air passes
beneath your words
and supports them on their way to my heart.
such a wind as this
can hold up the world
or blow clean the past
in a moment.

Video idea: Project images of an ocean, and then at the end of the poem, project the word "mighty" onto the screen; then fade away or transition to the next reading and set of images.

MATTHEW   i've been trying to find a term for you,
a way to pour your essence into a single word.
but a few letters can't contain you.
i can speak your name, but that's not enough.
you pour beyond the syllables like an ocean tipped into a thimble.

[Two-minute mark]

Video idea: Project images of a seashell or a blossoming flower and then at the end of the poem, project the word "prayer" onto the screen; then fade away or transition to the next reading and set of images.

CHERISE   sometimes you answer my prayers before i speak them;
before my heart even knows they're there.
and sometimes,
you let my dreams linger in my heart until
they burst into prayers that have no answers.
maybe you do it so we always have something to talk about—
either the answers or the questions.
i guess you're wise that way.
if you only gave me one or the other,
i might never have found you at all.

Video idea: Project images of a broken piece of pottery, then a beautiful vase and then in the middle of the poem, project the word "flawed" onto the screen; then at the end of the poem, project the word "grace" and fade away as you transition into worship music.

MATTHEW   i lift my prayer up to the light to see
if it's counterfeit after all.

CHERISE   i scan the lines of its text, i peer
              at the fabric and the texture.

MATTHEW   i turn it over and read the fine print.
              and then, sadly, i set it down,

CHERISE   "this one is as flawed as all the
              rest," i mumble.

[Three-minute mark]

MATTHEW   and i toss it onto
              the pile of my other discarded prayers.

CHERISE   but you look down and smile
              and say, by the grace in your heart,

MATTHEW   "ah, another true prayer has been offered today."

CHERISE   this is a mystery to me.

MATTHEW   i feel so counterfeit,
              yet you make me so real.

CHERISE   and i stumble over the words as i try
              to thank you again
              for being my God.

Exit. Fade out. Transition into a set of worship music.

APPENDIX 1

CHECKLIST FOR STRONG CHURCH DRAMAS

It's easy to find sketches to perform in church settings. There are hundreds (probably thousands) of free scripts online. All you have to do is download them and print them out. So, why another book of dramas?

Well, there's a reason those sketches are free: most of them aren't very good. Most of them are sermons in disguise, where one person has a problem and goes to the "wise answer giver" who shows his misguided friend the "error in his ways" and then leads him in a sinner's prayer so they can all live "happily ever after." While I don't know of a foolproof formula for writing good dramas, that's certainly a foolproof formula for writing a bad one.

Good dramas have characters and struggles we can relate to and give us questions to think about rather than answers we're supposed to believe. Here are a few guidelines for evaluating dramatic sketches.

- Does each character struggle with something? None of the characters should have all the answers. Every character should want something or have a goal or an unfulfilled desire that gives them a reason to be on stage.

- Does tension escalate until it reaches a conclusion that is both inevitable and unpredictable? A drama must move forward rather than simply de-escalate into a conversation or a two-person sermon. Even a disagreement isn't a drama—it's just the seed that could give birth to a drama. The more tension, the more drama. Very often, tension can arise because of strife between two people's conflicting goals.

- Is the ending predictable, or is it surprising? When a drama begins, listeners naturally and unconsciously begin to identify with one of the characters. We tend to identify with the character who seems to be like us. So I like to switch things around. Once the listeners are on the side of one of the characters, I like to pull the rug out from under them so that the story hits home. As soon as listeners can guess how a drama will end or how it will get to the end, they begin to lose interest.

- Does the drama move the listeners? Sketches do more than just entertain or inform people. They affect us. I believe our goal in drama ministry should be to speak the truth in a way that moves people to the place where they can encounter God. If all we're doing is informing people, we've failed. Explanations don't move people, stories do. We should strive to reach not just the intellect but also the imagination; not just the head but also the heart—just as Jesus did when he taught.

- Are the characters believable and three-dimensional? One-dimensional characters are either good or evil—one or the other. Believable characters are more like us—sorta good and sorta evil. Mixed up, flawed, hopeful, hopeless, concerned, distracted and real. (Note, there's one exception: In comedic sketches the characters are usually more shallow or stereotypical because humor exaggerates traits or characteristics in order to show us by overstatement how ludicrous we sometimes act.)

- Are the characters people the audience can identify with? Age, background, interests and so forth affect how well the audience can identify with dramatic characters. The more we have in common with them, the easier it will be to identify with them. The more we can identify with the different characters and their struggles and discoveries, the more we'll be drawn into the story.

- Is the blocking natural rather than forced? Movement should not arise from contrived situations but from the natural interaction of the characters with their environment. As you read the scripts aloud with your actors (especially once they've learned their lines), you'll notice places where movement becomes instinctive. That's good because the more gestures and blocking appear to be rehearsed, the less effective they are. So strive to be natural and responsive rather than wooden and canned.

- Is dialogue natural-sounding? Well-written dialogue is crafted aloud rather than on paper. You can usually tell by reading it. Are the sentences long, complex, stilted and grammatically correct? Or is the language abrupt, conversational and informal?

- Overall, does the drama reinforce Christian clichés, or does it replace them? Effective dramas show us our blind spots rather than make them larger.

- Does the drama offer the audience a chance to ask meaningful questions? If no questions are raised, it is probably not a very effective script.

APPENDIX 2

HINTS FOR ACTORS

Whenever you act out a scene, you're doing two things simultaneously—remembering and responding. At the same time you're remembering your lines, you're also responding to the other characters, the setting, the action and the audience.

Remembering and responding work together so that when they're done well, the audience notices neither. So rehearse to respond. Practice until everything becomes natural enough so that you can respond to what's going on without being distracted by trying to remember your lines. Your lines need to become second nature. If you have to spend your attention or mental energy remembering your lines, you won't say them naturally. You won't be totally present in the moment.

So when you approach a script, spend less time and effort trying to "get it right" and spend more time trying to absorb the words so that you can act out the scene in a way that frees you up to respond naturally to the other people on stage.

Since you want your movement and gestures to grow naturally from your interaction with the text of the script, don't memorize with your mind. Memorize with your body. Experience the words as you rehearse them. Walk and move your way through the script. Let the setting and the interaction with the other people on stage help you develop your gestures and actions. Also remember to

- Pour emotion into action. Don't act out what you're feeling. Instead, show by what you do how those feelings make you respond.

- Be aware. Step into the role and notice what's going on. Be prepared to find what you're not looking for.

- Learn your lines on time. If the rest of the of the cast has learned their lines and you haven't, you're wasting their time. Learning your lines is a sign of respect and an integral part of this type of ministry.

- Respond with spontaneity. Respond to what's happening now, regardless of how things are supposed to go or how they went in rehearsal. Learn to listen with your eyes and then respond with your body.

APPENDIX 3

SUGGESTED SEGUES

Weaving together a cohesive worship service can be difficult. It's tough to find the thread of imagery or meaning that ties together the music, message and drama in a way that makes sense but isn't overly didactic.

Often, the more you explain a story the less impact it has, so it's not always essential to explain the dramas or their connection to the message. However, transitions between the drama and the music or message are often handled poorly. It's important to retain the right tone and not undermine what was said.

Listed below are possible segues that the speaker or preacher could use to transition into the message. Use them as springboards to create your own seamless worship services.

Not What I Expected

Let's be honest for a minute. Usually the way heaven is described at most churches, it doesn't sound all that exciting. It kinda resembles a never-ending church service. Let's just say it—it sounds boring. Thankfully, that's not the picture the Bible gives us of heaven. A place of boredom, regret and tedium is much more like the place down below.

The Commentator

James, the brother of Jesus once wrote, "Do not merely listen to the word, and so deceive yourselves. Do what it says" (James 1:22 NIV). I heard of a monk long ago who prayed, "God, don't teach me anything new until I've learned to put into practice what I already know." At first it sounds like a foolish prayer. But I think it's an incredibly brave and honest one. God doesn't want a *yes* spoken with your mouth; he wants a *yes* spoken with your life. I wonder how many of us would be brave enough to pray that prayer today.

Astray

(Tell a brief personal story about someone you've known who forgot who he was in Christ. How did it affect his life? What happened? What can we do to better remember our spiritual identity?)

Being Human

(You may want to transition directly into a set of worship music. If you decide to address the audience, walk on stage as the actors exit and face the audience. Then as the lights come back up, say something like "I've spent a good chunk of my life asking that very question—who am I? And how do I fit into this mixed up, wounded, wonderful world?")

Cravings

What do you crave? What do you desire? If you're like most of us, you want to live happily ever after, but you just don't really know how to get there. (In your message, emphasize the hope and fulfillment we can have through the reality of Christ—John 10:10.)

Virgo

Your convictions, your values, your beliefs—where do they come from? Your parents? Culture? MTV? Talk radio? The church you went to as a kid? Being a follower of Jesus involves more than going to church or following certain rules. It involves pursuing purity for the right reasons and rooting your convictions in the life and teachings of your Master.

Love Thy Neighbor

I wonder how I would react if Jesus just showed up at the coffee shop, the video store or the front door of our church. I wonder what I would do if I found out the homeless guy I'd just ignored was really Jesus in disguise. (Explore Matthew 25:31-46).

No Trespassing

If you're anything like me, you're probably glad there's no such thing as thought police. Imagine if you could get arrested for impure thoughts. Imagine living in a world where you were accountable not only for what you do but also for what you think. Well guess what? According to Jesus, that is the kind of world we live in.

Welcome to MAG ONE

Too many accountability groups and small group Bible studies are just like MAG ONE. No one is really transparent, and no one is really transformed. Humility and honesty lie at the heart of Christianity. Jesus calls us to stop hiding and to be honest with God and with each other. The question for us is, Are we ready to walk that road or not?

The Phone Call

Most marital problems start as spiritual problems. Discontentment and frustration grow not just because we're drifting away from our spouse, but because we're drifting away from our Lord.

Too Late

Lots of times there are no easy answers to life's biggest questions. None of this surprises Jesus. After all, he experienced some of those questions for himself.

Apology Accepted

Why is it so hard to say those two words—*I'm sorry*? Why are they the two hardest words of all to say—both to others and to God? What gets in the way of us saying those two simple words?

The Kingdom

Jesus turned religion on its head when he talked about the kingdom of heaven. He didn't always explain himself but let his stories speak for themselves. Even today, we need to let his stories sink into our souls and then change us from the inside out.

Bigger Barns

I guess in the end, most all of us get caught building bigger barns. We just have different names for them.

The Fire Within

(You may want to transition directly into a set of worship music. If you decide to address the audience, you may wish to say something like this . . .) Genuine worship isn't something that's easy to define or describe. Faith is a mystery. The apostle Paul called Jesus "the mystery of God, . . . in whom are hidden all the treasures of wisdom and knowledge" (Colossians 2:2-3 NIV). And remember, Jesus called himself "the truth" (John 14:6). He is both *mystery* and *truth*, together in one person. The pathway to truth lies through the heart of the mystery of Jesus.

Don't be afraid of mystery. As soon as you try to divorce mystery from Christianity, you kill it. Worshiping a God we cannot see is the most mysterious, refreshing and essential act of all.

Cast Index

Sketches for One Male and One Female

Apology Accepted

The Commentator

Not What I Expected

The Phone Call

Ripples in the Divine Sea

Virgo

Sketches for Two Males

Love Thy Neighbor

Too Late

Sketches for Two Males and Two Females

The Kingdom

Sketches for Three (Males or Females)

The Fire Within

No Trespassing

Sketches for Four (Males or Females)

Astray

Bigger Barns (optional fifth person)

Sketches for Five (Males or Females)

Being Human

Bigger Barns (optional fifth person)

Cravings

Sketches for Five Males

Welcome to MAG ONE

Topical Index

The Kingdom
Love Thy Neighbor
Not What I Expected . . .
Ripples in the Divine Sea
Virgo

Modern Life
Bigger Barns
The Commentator
The Kingdom

Obedience
The Commentator
No Trespassing

Pain
Astray
Too Late

Prayer
The Fire Within
Ripples in the Divine Sea

Priorities
Bigger Barns
The Kingdom
No Trespassing
Too Late
Virgo

Purity
Cravings
No Trespassing
The Phone Call
Virgo

Questions
Astray
Being Human
Too Late

Relationships
Apology Accepted

Love Thy Neighbor
Virgo

Religion
The Fire Within
Love Thy Neighbor

Self-Control
Cravings
No Trespassing
The Phone Call
Virgo

Self-Esteem
Astray

Self-Indulgence
Bigger Barns
Cravings

Sex
Virgo

Sin
Apology Accepted
Being Human
Cravings
No Trespassing

Spirituality
The Commentator
The Fire Within
The Kingdom
Ripples in the Divine Sea

Suffering
Too Late

Suicide
Astray

Temptation
Being Human

Cravings
No Trespassing
The Phone Call
Virgo

Thought Life
No Trespassing
The Phone Call
Welcome to MAG ONE

Truth
Apology Accepted
Love Thy Neighbor
Too Late

Valuing Life
Too Late

Witnessing
The Fire Within
Love Thy Neighbor

Wonder
Astray
The Fire Within
Ripples in the Divine Sea

Worship
The Fire Within
Ripples in the Divine Sea

Scripture Index